Association for Middle Level Educati

ELYSE S. SCOTT

Awakening the Middle School Voice:

Engineering the Language Arts to Excite Adolescents

Library of Congress Control Number: 2015950231

"The art of teaching is the art of assisting discovery."
—Mark Van Doren

Dedication

To all my middle school students who took their journey
of discovery with me and to my granddaughter Jillian who endures
my endless questions about her middle school experiences!

With thanks,

Mrs. S

About the Author

Elyse S. Scott is a retired English teacher who began her career teaching at the community college level but found her true passion: teaching middle school. With over thirty years of experience teaching at the middle level, she served as mentor for new teachers and cooperating teacher for many student teachers. Her years as an eighth grade team leader gave her invaluable insights into the realities of the multi-dimensional experience unique to middle level education. With wit and wisdom, she writes about what she learned as her career progressed and through decades of guiding teachers through their sometimes overwhelming challenges in the middle. She now writes and consults in the Hudson Valley of New York. See her other book from AMLE, *Secrets from the Middle: Making Who You Are Work for You*.

Table of Contents

Author's Note. iii

Introduction vii

Chapter 1   Why Awaken the Middle School Voice? 1

Chapter 2   In the Beginning 7

Chapter 3   A Good Story. 19

Chapter 4   The Novelty of Novels. 35

Chapter 5   Midterms? Let's Get Creative!. 59

Chapter 6   Author Seminar 65

Chapter 7   Let's Get Published! 73

Chapter 8   Fight Spring Fever with Poetry 87

Chapter 9   To the Finish Line 101

Chapter 10   What About Reading and Writing Instruction? . . . 105

"Balance is beautiful."
—Miyoko Ohno

Introduction

A friend and former educator upon completing my first book *Secrets from the Middle: Making Who You Are Work For You* remarked, "I loved it, but I'd love to see your lesson plans!" My reply: "I'm on it!"

As I write this book, the debate over the Common Core Standards rages on. Having studied the English Language Arts standards in depth, I will not argue against their intent. It is very difficult to rant against rigor, high expectations, and preparedness for the future for all students. In fact, as a teacher in New York state for more than 30 years, I feel my state adopted a set of high standards well over a decade ago, and I worked very diligently to align my curriculum to those standards. What I will argue against is any attempt to have students frustrated and discouraged because their individual needs and stages of development do not coincide with those standards. I do argue against a standardized testing system that does not truly reflect what students and teachers do on an ongoing basis. I also argue that over-reliance on prescribed learning modules stifles creativity and flexibility, the hallmarks of a true learning community.

As in all things, I advocate balance. The Common Core standards are just that—"standards"; they are not a rigid curriculum. They allow for a great deal of teacher "engineering" to meet the needs, and most importantly, the interests of students. If they remind us that we should be tapping into our students' critical thinking skills, fostering inquiry and project-based learning, and doing more writing than ever, then that is a good thing. However, it is the classroom teacher whose professional judgment determines what will best meet the needs of students: capturing their interest, deepening their understanding, and extending their thinking.

Above all, I always wanted my students to be excited about learning, and once I got them hooked by choosing wonderful, relevant materials, even the most reticent among them became contributing voices!

Chapter 1

"I thank you for your voices:
thank you: Your most sweet voices."
—William Shakespeare

Why Awaken the Middle School Voice?

Middle school voices are not always what their teachers want to hear. Those voices can be high-pitched and rowdy, full of criticism and negativity, whining with complaint, or bent on distracting others, destroying the most well-intentioned lesson. So why would we want to "awaken the middle school voice"? The answer is that the most glorious middle school voices can be dormant, in recesses that even students themselves did not know existed. Once unleashed they can be truly powerful, and once redirected, capitalize on those very qualities that often give adolescents a bad name. Once transformed, negative energy can translate to strength of conviction, enthusiasm, cleverness, and dynamism. Classes once branded "unruly," "zoo-ish," "dysfunctional" transform into learning communities in which collaboration and an open exchange of ideas are routine.

Thirty years ago I began my middle school journey teaching English full of the best intentions. I was organized, planned my lessons meticulously, and was full of high ideals about what adolescents needed. What did I really know when I entered my classroom for the first time: some background on adolescents from education courses that could never prepare me for my real life encounters in the classroom, field observations of other teachers' students, and an all too limited engagement student teaching. I taught "the way I had been taught" and stayed one step ahead of the students. I gave the kind of tests I had been given, as well as similar papers and projects.

But as my career progressed, my students themselves would come to inform the changes I would make in instruction, approach, content, projects, and most important, who I was as their teacher. You cannot last long with middle school students doing "the same old, same old." Adolescents can be painfully blunt, and they will tell you when things are not working. Luckily, my gut instincts were victorious before my students rebelled. As young teachers we tend to focus on ourselves, but slowly my focus started to shift to my students, their interests, their needs.

In a caseload of middle school students, there will always be the respectful "worker bees" as we used to call them, but many students, then and now, shuffle into class after class, take a seat, and bear an expression that translates into something like, "Well, teacher, give me your best shot." Long before all the technological distractions of today, middle school students were "checking out" in increasing numbers. If you sat in the wings and listened to middle school students complain about their teachers and classes, which they did, and still do all the time, you could glean some important information. Often you would hear comments like, "She always does the same old thing," "He spends two weeks on one story," "She talks and talks and talks, and we just sit there," "We read half the book in class; I want to read it on my own!" "He's very nice, but class is so boring," with a huge dramatic pronunciation of "b-o-r-i-n-g." I really opened my ears, as well as my mind and heart, to what kids were saying, and as good teachers always do, examined my own practices.

I realized early on that in order to make a difference, I had to be different. I had to be dynamic and energetic, and the only way I could be those things was if I loved what I was teaching. I had to embrace the material I was presenting. Literary works had to resonate with me, and I had to develop a sixth sense for what would work with my students. I often used the students as guinea pigs for some materials, and gave them some control by having them give a thumbs up or down, with a rationale, of course. As an English teacher, I had limitless resources from which to choose, but my criteria for adoption had to include relevancy in some way for my students. I also had to decide what my priorities were. If my main mission was to aid my students in discovery, promote a lifelong love of reading and writing, and tap their critical insights, then my own "inner curriculum map" had to include inspiring materials carefully engineered to get students hooked and to be active participants. I would have to create models of my own design that would suggest alternate paths for my students who were caught in ruts of sameness. Projects, assignments, and assessments would have to be authentic, exciting, and fun. My questioning, whether to the class or on assessments, had to be thought-provoking, challenging, mind-boggling, even, to elicit student voices capable of sharing wisdom and insight, formulating arguments and making judgments, critically analyzing and evaluating.

Even as standards and testing mania hit the middle level, I had to find a happy medium in preparing my students for assessments while staying true to the heart of my classroom—tapping students' voices, creativity, and critical thinking. I did not have to "throw the baby out with the bath water" and start anew. I had been using wonderful materials all along; I just approached them with new perspective, adding and subtracting as student interest and perspective changed from year to year. We have all heard the saying, "What's old can be new again," and that became my mantra as I massaged and tweaked old standbys that still had merit. I allowed content to be the vehicle of inspiration, embedding demanded skills rather than having the skills themselves be the lesson headliners.

All too often, I have noted that teachers plan their lessons as though they were laying out a buffet table—a sampling of this, a taste of that—too many loose ends that keep students foggy about purpose and relevance. Those of us who teach language arts, while often complaining how comprehensive and multi-stranded our standards are, also have wide flexibility in choice of materials, sequence of instruction, and types of projects and assessments.

Lately I have been hearing an outcry about literature being put aside in favor of the non-fiction and otherwise "neutral" text that students will encounter on standardized tests. Avoid the temptation at all costs! While there is wonderful non-fiction that will excite and inspire middle school students, literature allows adolescents to take emotional risks, respond authentically, and raise questions. This book is a result of a transformed educational philosophy. When teachers become facilitators of learning and students are vested stakeholders, possibilities are endless. I share with you the fruits of constantly going back to the proverbial "drawing board" with my eighth graders through the years. The ideas and suggestions, though, can easily be streamlined and adapted for grades six and seven as well. There is truly only one method to awaken the middle school voice. The path begins by buying into the adolescent world and its demands. It's not about giving in; it's about giving up the old "ties that bind." The payoff is you won't be hearing the voices in your head telling you something is not working, but you will be hearing the voices of your students having something profound to say!

I have organized this book just as I often organized my year for English Language Arts Grade 8. I would allow the content to arouse student interest and get them excited, then I would "engineer" the material to achieve my goals for my students. The content would provide the springboard for teaching demanded skills, writing topics, and critical thinking.

Chapter 2

"The beginning is the most important part of the work."
—Plato

In the Beginning

For most teachers the beginning of each school year is fraught with meetings, to-do lists, attendance printouts, and schedule changes. Despite supreme organization at the end of the summer, those initial details seem to derail the best laid plans of even the most organized veteran teacher. This preliminary anxiety can stall teachers in their goal to get to know their students immediately, which is paramount in beginning as quickly as possible to tap student voice, creativity, and critical thinking. From the very first days, exercises, writing prompts, and projects can be the springboards for awakening students from their summer lethargy, and they speak volumes about students' abilities, creativity quotients, and critical thinking skills.

From that first day in a teacher's classroom, students get a vibe that tells them whether a class will be one they look forward to or will eventually earn a boring rating. If teachers want the best their students have to give—insightful and thoughtful discussions, original and creative work, excellent writing—then teachers must be the wellspring of those very things. Every teacher has a gift, and if possible, should present that gift on the very first day. As a poet, I delivered my rules and regulations, my pet peeves and my likes, and some personal info via a rhyming poem. It worked for me because I love to write poetry, and it allowed me to inject my sense of humor and show my students a clever way to get some very important information across. Now not everyone writes poetry. Some teachers are great storytellers.

Some teachers are great artists—to share a sketch, or cartoon, or painting is to reveal a side of their being that will not only dazzle students but reveal a part of their soul. When teachers share their gifts—their human being side—pathways and connections are opened immediately. Students see that this might well be a place where their gifts will be appreciated as well.

That is why, if at all possible, teachers should put aside pre- and diagnostic tests, and plunge right into work that immediately establishes community and reveals the unique abilities of each student. The legwork begun in those early days will lay the groundwork for a richer, more collaborative classroom environment.

Beyond "What I Did On My Summer Vacation"

That age-old writing prompt had a purpose in those first days of a new school year. It got students writing and gave a bit of insight into who they were as kids. I used it or something similar until I realized it told me only part of the story, perhaps something about writing skills and a tad about my students' personalities. Later, that gave way to an autobiography, usually in a five-part format. However, my teaching sense, and I'll admit, a certain boredom in reading close to 125 of these things, led me to create a mini-project that was exciting for both my students and me.

I started by explaining the purpose of the project—I needed to get to know my students as people so I could really connect to them and successfully teach them. As I had introduced myself through poetry, I wanted them to choose a creative way to introduce themselves to me. I also quoted Lao Tzu, "He who knows others is wise; he who knows himself is enlightened." Doing this assignment would be more than fulfilling an obligation; they would be learning something about themselves in the process.

It started with choice. I gave students options from which to choose the best vehicle for presenting their own life stories. Now there would always be those students who wanted the comfort of a known quantity so they would choose to do a traditional autobiography. That told me something about them right away; that they would have to ease into more creative approaches, perhaps with a gentle nudge from the teacher. These might be students who preferred the comfort zone, but time would tell. From the rest of the students came immediate discussion and excitement about which option they might choose.

- Write a poem capturing all the elements that make you "you."

- Create a collage that captures the "symbols of your life." In an oral presentation or writing, share the story behind these symbols.

- Design a scrapbook that incorporates written and visual representations of who you are.

- Allow some form of technology to be the framework for your life story, for example, a PowerPoint presentation or video.

- Invent your own project (collaborate with teacher before proceeding).

The students had a few days to complete the assignment. Meanwhile, in addition to the poem I had written, I shared my own collage, and I modeled the kind of presentation expected, thoroughness of explanation, excellent voice. I had also written a story about a very unhappy teenager who hated school but later became a teacher, and I read it to the class. I left out until the end that the narrator was actually me. I showed them that this was a different direction but certainly revealed much about my past and who I am.

The results were amazing. Students were excited about their own products, but equally enthusiastic about seeing and hearing about their classmates' work as well. Only a few days into the school year, students were already focusing on writing, artistic expression, and ingenuity. I was thrilled to have all kinds of work to assess rather than the huge stack of the usual essays.

The most wonderful payoff of all, though, was the range of invention and originality. Some teachers worry about modeling for students because they fear it will narrow what students do. I always found the opposite was true. It gave students some wiggle room to try something different; I was just giving them other ways of looking at the same assignment. Students paired up and interviewed each other and produced magazine-like articles. There were poetry books, art pieces, CDs of songs that students felt mirrored their lives, which they played and explained the significance of. There were one-man shows by students who loved the spotlight and talking about their favorite subjects—them. From podcasts to brochures to videotaped talk shows, my students fulfilled the assignment in ways I never even thought to suggest.

In one week our class had become a learning community. The students knew their teacher had worked just as hard as they did, valued their ability to make their own choices, and recognized that a diverse group might just capitalize on diverse options. Students shared their work with one another, rather than simply heading to the collection pile with only one "person in the audience." They, in turn, gave me tons of information that would come to inform instruction, as well as future assignments and projects.

What's In a Name?

All adolescents are narcissistic to some degree, which is why this project is so appealing. Students love to write about themselves, but in writing about their names, they have so many angles from which to approach the topic: derivation—why parents chose their name, feelings associated with the name, both positive and negative. The assignment required one page only and each page would be compiled into a Book of Names of all my students that year. Thus, the excitement began. Students were thrilled to graduate from the old acrostic of their name with descriptors of each letter that was often an early assignment in some class. They wanted to know if they could draw, use clip art, veer from MLA format on fonts and colors—and, of course, the answer was an unequivocal, "YES!" By way of modeling, I read them "My Name" from *The House on Mango Street* (Cisneros, 1984) in which Esperanza shares her feelings about being given her great-grandmother's name, and I shared my own (and I recommend that you try it as well).

Example

Elyse

For almost twenty years of my life, I resented my name. I was always the odd duck without a cool name like the Barbaras and

Robyns and Lynns of my time. "Elyse" was a strange one with a strange spelling, and people just never got it right. Teachers would call me Elsie, and though there is really nothing wrong with that name, it just so happens it is not mine. I had enough self-esteem issues years ago to qualify for first-class basket case status. Having a name that was different caused me endless anxiety. It wasn't enough that I was shy, awkward, chubby, unsure of myself, I had to have a name that made people pause and put me under a magnifying glass. The irony is that my mother named me after some long-gone movie star, Elyse Knox. No way did I identify with celebrity status. But what is life without irony? As I got older, people would comment on my name: "lovely," "different," "It's French, isn't it?" You just never know in this life. Perhaps, I grew into the name. Or perhaps, as I gained self-confidence, I came to embrace it. But it is now simply a part of me, like my brown eyes, my pathetic sense of humor, or my penchant for shoes and bling.

This is a great short project to do in computer lab or an assignment to be completed in a few days. A built-in bonus is that it encourages students to sit down with their parents for background information, and parents love to be a part of what's going on in class. Again, students were ecstatic because they had control over approach and design, and when it came time to turn in the pages, almost everyone shared either by reading out loud or by presenting their pages on the document camera. Although it was only the beginning of the school year, students were participating, collaborating on approach, and designing beautiful pieces. We "published" them all in a binder of glossy sleeves, and I even invited students to create a cover for our book, later voting on the one that would have the place of honor. Over the course of the year, that book got manhandled because students loved to read the work of others, and, of course, to see their names in print. I received the biggest dividend of all. I got to see what kind of paths my students would take in the project, the range of writing skills for an authentic piece, and an aspect of their personal profile that I might have simply glossed over on the attendance list.

While my goal as a teacher at the middle level was to assist my students in discovering their own inventiveness, one eye was always trained on the standards. These initial projects, though fun and creative, were also requiring students to produce writing in which development, organization, word choice, and style were appropriate to task, purpose, and audience.

So, What Do You Think?

Just as important as getting your students to write, create, and contribute as early as possible is tapping their thinking skills. From the outset, you want to know what kind of thinkers they are. First off, are they curious? Are they independent problem solvers? Are they logical thinkers? Are they critical analyzers? Do they think metaphorically? Can they make inferences, predictions, and judgments?

From the first day that students walked into my class, without them knowing it, I was assessing what kind of thinkers they were. I tested their curiosity quotient by having interesting artwork and photographs around the room. I would wait to see who was the first person to ask me about a poster-size photo of me with a monkey on my head. Then I would ask them to come up with theories of how this ape landed on my head. Actually, it was a Barbary Ape on the Rock of Gibraltar (with a gamekeeper right at my side but not in the photo) but the side-splitting explanations from my students were incredible, especially the one from a student who said I had used banana scented shampoo and the monkey found me irresistible! Souvenirs from my travels, family pictures, my *I Love Lucy* and golf memorabilia (which students added to over my entire career), former students' drawings and small projects—all elicited comments and questions from my new students who had pretty much decided this teacher was worth getting to know better.

I always wrote a quote on the board, and when possible, I chose the quote for its relevance to what we were studying in class. I also put little brain teasers on the board, and students would beg for more. Most important, I "formally" assessed each student's thinking abilities within the first few weeks of class. I found that with a carefully selected prompt, I could tell a great deal about my students' critical thinking skills and their ability to express their insights. A paragraph or two in response to a question would speak volumes about their thought processes. The key, though, was that I chose these prompts initially for their ability to pique my students' interest; their analysis of more sophisticated material would come later. I always kept an eye out for short pieces that were humorous, inspiring, weird, or controversial—or all of those. My sources ranged from interesting news articles to excerpts from Chicken Soup books to Internet tidbits like Bill Gates' "11 Rules of Life." I asked questions like: What is the author's purpose? What does the author want us to learn about life? What connections can you make to...? What evidence can you find that...? How do you know...?

By the End of the Beginning

It was phenomenal how much information I was able to collect about each of my students in just a few weeks. After numerous writing samples, two projects, and endless opportunities to raise their critical awareness, I felt that we were already a thriving learning community in which my students were vested stakeholders. Yes, I had done my share in terms of work required to get to that place, but the energy, enthusiasm, and creativity of my students was the payoff.

By this time and throughout the year, I would use these assignments and projects to zero in on writing skills rather than treat them in isolation. When I found common errors (which I continuously did) I put them on the board on the day I returned graded work. Though faces and names changed from year to year, writing errors remained fairly consistent. Number One in eighth grade tended to be what I dubbed, "the dreaded run-on." Middle school students tend to attach thoughts with "and" until they have a one paragraph sentence or they attach everything with commas in rampant comma splices. That would lead us to the bogeyman of all punctuation marks for my students: the use of the semicolon. By focusing on these errors in context of the assignment at hand, I found my students improved so much more than through isolated exercises from a grammar text or worksheet. In addition, I always tried to show them model responses, essays, and projects so we could analyze what made them exemplars.

I found that mini-lessons on all aspects of writing were far more helpful continuously throughout the year rather than a writing unit that might serve as the basis for writing expectations, rarely to be returned to. Middle school students needed that constant reinforcement, and they were very enthusiastic about the process.

A Word About Grading

As educators we tend to get hung up on the grading of our students' creative endeavors. At the beginning of the year I was not as concerned about rubrics, though it would not be difficult to create them. I treated most of the work at the beginning as individual expression, and my comments to each student were so appreciated. I wrote notes of encouragement and pointed out areas that could be strengthened, and unless a student showed little or no effort, I tended to be lenient with grades since we all have to have those "letters or numbers" for report card time.

For short responses and extended paragraphs, I introduced students early on to a rubric similar to that used on New York state tests, which dealt with insight and critical thinking content as opposed to written elements and mechanics. Many of my colleagues used it as well. Using the rubric allowed students to internalize the elements necessary in writing about critical thought. I used it often for many of the short prompts and topics I mention in ensuing chapters.

Rubric for ELA Tasks

6   Entirely correct, sophisticated, insightful response/ demonstrates a complete and thorough understanding of the task maintaining a clear focus/makes connections and demonstrates reflection using accurate and relevant examples from text or film/vivid language and challenging vocabulary

5   Essentially correct/lacks the consistent quality of a 6/shows slightly less understanding/less elaboration

4   Focused/readable/with minor inaccuracies/simple sentences/ basic vocabulary

3   Partial understanding/incomplete, sketchy responses/gaps in understanding

2   Readable but not logical/inaccuracies/fragmented thoughts

1   Very brief/confused/lack of understanding

0   Incorrect/incoherent/irrelevant

Even though I scored the papers from 6 down to 0, I also made comments and corrections. Students need to have their work validated each and every time. My colleagues on my team adopted this rubric for written pieces in their classes as well and worked hard to show students exemplars and work in need of improvement in their content areas.

****(note-my school used numerical grades; therefore, a 6=100, 5=90, 4=80, and so on. At times I might give a 5–6, 4–5, or 3–4 if students were on the edge of a particular level, thus equating to 95, 85, 75 respectively.)

Chapter 3

"The universe is made of stories, not of atoms."
—Muriel Ruckeyser

A Good Story

All children love a good story, but adolescents and the short story are the perfect combination.

On the most practical level, short stories are doable in class. Some teachers do a short story unit that incorporates a number of stories. Each story generates a vocabulary list on which students are quizzed, questions that students must answer, and, perhaps, superficial discussion. This is truly a lost opportunity and only scratches at the surface of deep learning. Likewise, using one story over a long period to teach a multitude of skills related to this genre tends to dull student interest.

If inspiring students, awakening their insights, and getting them to think deeply are paramount, then the short story is the perfect format. Of course, a short story unit allows the teacher to discuss the elements of literature, for example, conflict, plot, setting, and in-context vocabulary. However, I have had students "parrot" types of conflict such as person vs. person, person vs. self, or identify the time and place of a story without seeing below the surface to the true significance of these elements. But when you truly get students to see how stories mirror the human condition, raise the universal questions of our existence, and explore the emotions and motives of characters, another part of their being is awakened. This does not happen instantaneously. I spent a great deal of time impressing upon my students that authors put their hearts and souls into the life lessons behind their stories. Many suffer for their art, and there is no shortage of writers' life stories full of addiction and drama that will enthrall middle school students. Thus, we, as their audience, must get past the one-line morals or "fortune cookie responses," as I was known to call them, to see into the soul of the writer and what we could learn about life.

I could not expect students, especially my most concrete thinkers, to take that leap into deep analysis without taking small steps first. I had to devise ways to lead them to this way of thinking. So I began with what I knew would arouse their interest, and in some cases, what they already knew.

Story Shorts

I began our discussion of the short story with a little exercise that would get students thinking about the genre and what makes it unique. Story shorts are one-liners, and though skeletal in nature, reveal the kernel of conflict that gets stories rolling. Students usually have that "ah ha" moment as they then add the details that we later realize are plot, character, and setting. These minis abound on the Internet, but here are some examples of what I used that really got students talking. Often I had students work in groups to fill in the details; they loved it.

- Rained, rained, rained, and never stopped.
- He read his obituary with confusion.

- Failed SAT. Lost scholarship. Invented rocket.
- The alleged Hemingway short: For sale: baby shoes, never worn.

~~Then we would graduate~~ to the ~~shortest stories I could find that would allow us to uncover themes despite such abbrevi~~ated ~~cont~~ent. Students loved these little nuggets! This is a favorite.

> In a crowded marketplace in Baghdad, a young servant was admiring colorful bolts of cotton fabric. Suddenly, a hooded female figure bumped into him. When the servant looked into the eyes of the dark figure, terror filled his heart. Quickly, he pushed his way through the crowd and fled. White and trembling, the servant returned home. He cried, "Just now in the marketplace a woman in the crowd jostled me. When I turned, I saw that the woman was Death! She made a threatening gesture. Please," the servant pleaded, "lend me your horse and I will ride away from this city. I will go to Samarra, where Death cannot find me." The master was fond of the servant and agreed to lend him his swiftest steed. The servant dug his spurs into the horse's flanks and, as fast as the horse could gallop, he went. Later that afternoon, the master went down to the marketplace. He saw Death standing in the crowd. "Why did you threaten my servant this morning?" he asked. "That was not a threatening gesture," responded Death. "It was a start of surprise. I was astonished to see him in Baghdad." "Astonished?" "Yes. You see, I have an appointment with him tonight…in Samarra."
> —Adapted from a retelling by W. Somerset Maugham

For some reason this story really resonated with my students, and though an ancient tale, they saw parallels in modern life.

Of course, knowing I was looking for depth, some character in the class would always offer as the meaning, "You can't escape death!" However, as our discussion moved along, students would grasp that not even with powerful friends can we outwit our fate. Adolescents are constantly grappling with their questions about death, and many were honest about their fears. They easily identified with the young servant and his conflict. My goal with this story and the following one, was to show them the multi-dimensional nature of theme analysis. I wanted them to see that even the shortest of stories can have depth of meaning.

One of the South's shortest ghost stories.

> This man was walkin' through a dark wood, a wood that folks said was haunted by evil spirits who took any mortal who came their way. But the man kept telling himself: I am a good man and have done no wrong. If evil spirits can harm me, then there isn't any justice. A voice behind the man said, "There isn't."
> —From *Ghost Stories from the American South.*

In this story most of my students saw that life is not always fair, and justice is not always served. They also saw that we all share fears—some of the dark, some of evil spirits. Most of all, though, we came to the conclusion that despite our best efforts as human beings to live well and do the right thing, the outcome is not always favorable despite our best intentions.

Childhood Revisited

When students saw Shel Silverstein's *The Giving Tree* in my hand, memories of childhood would come rushing back to them. Filled with nostalgia, they would ask why I had it. Once I had their attention, I explained that middle school students tend to see the author's purpose as a moral captured in a sentence or two. But together I wanted us to uncover truths, real implications, life lessons we could take away from our reading. And so with rapt attention they would listen as I read this classic from their past. The discussion that ensued was even more gratifying. We went beyond the importance of truth telling and the pitfalls of selfishness vs. gratitude. Students explored the relationship implications of give and take, honor, and respect. They delved into consequence of actions, growth, and maturity, and they even talked about the "what ifs" of our lives. I capitalized on their experience with this analysis, explaining that even the shortest of stories has much to teach us about life, and our collective insights constituted "theme," not some moral that could fit on a fortune cookie strip of paper. Reading a children's book or two goes a long way in promoting deeper understanding of the short story.

Writer's Purpose

Next, I wanted students to examine material that was familiar to them. Adolescents have their favorite songs, shows that they never miss, movies that they watch over and over, and poems they hold close to the heart. I asked them to choose one of these (appropriate material only), and in a well-written response, explain the writer's purpose. I reminded them that all of these forms—from songs to TV shows begin with the writer. On the day the assignment was due, I placed the song lyrics and poems on the document camera, and students analyzed their chosen work; classmates then added their insights.

The class discussed movies and television shows in open forum. How can I describe the exchange of ideas that took place during that lesson? Wisdom, maturity, depth of understanding—these materials were relevant to my students' worlds, and it showed in their analyses. The most valuable outcome of this assignment was that students with more concrete interpretations had their eyes opened by their peers to new possibilities of meaning. Then, we would use that same approach in making the leap to a mainstream short story.

Group Analysis with a Wide-Angle Lens

Up to this point, students demonstrated that they well understood various conflicts, the effect of time and place on a story, and characterization techniques. A good portion of the class was now stronger in analyzing themes. But old habits die hard and superficial thinking often prevailed. This is where group analysis can be powerful in uncovering an author's purpose(s). Students get to listen to one another's thinking, and the dialogue that ensues is incredibly insightful. I often asked students to report on their thinking. How did they read between the lines? What clues could they find in the story? How did they reach their conclusions? Learning to think about their thinking is a valuable skill.

Example 1: Richard Peck's "Priscilla and the Wimps"

It can be read in a few minutes, lends itself to fantastic oral interpretation which always gave me a lift, and kids are hooked at the first sentence. Opportunities for deep thinking abound with such questions as

> In what way is the story a satire?
>
> From whose point of view is the story told?
>
> What information are you given about this person?
>
> What is the significance of setting?

However, the reason I would have groups work on author's purpose was to get beyond the typical adolescent response that "you shouldn't bully anyone." I would have groups record all the possibilities that came up in their conversation and then report out. I would record their responses and most times, it would look something like this.

- Victims of bullies are scared and go along because they have no choice

- Schools need to be safe where staff members are the authority figures

- Stereotypes are not always valid

- Karma- sometimes there is justice

- Life is full of irony

Example 2: Katharine Brush's "Birthday Party"

Again an analysis of the importance of setting, point of view, conflict, and character makes for interesting discussion, but middle school students have a difficult time with Brush. It is challenging to get adolescents past how mean the husband is to his poor wife, and how ungrateful he is. However, as students flesh out what the narrator is feeling and start examining the husband/wife relationship, they begin to see beyond their initial reactions. They start asking questions like,

- Why does the wife surprise him when it seems he's the type that wouldn't like it?

- Shouldn't these people know each other better after being married so long?

- Why can't the husband just suck it up?

- How can this wife go on being so miserable?

Students learn through the exercise that a seemingly short, short story has so much to say about all the issues that comprise relationships, empathy for other human beings, and even has them forecasting whether this marriage will endure.

I always explained that this "wide angle lens" that the group used is an important tool that individual students can use to improve their own writing. Using this process and then filling in supporting details from the story would yield an intelligent discussion of an author's purpose. The key was learning to never settle for only one way of looking at an author's work.

Fun Friday!

Years ago, long before language arts included listening as a strand of the curriculum, I invented a listening exercise to keep my Fridays somewhat sane. Middle school students can be crazed on Fridays especially if there is a ski trip planned or a big game on the weekend. As I read an interesting news article (truth is often stranger than fiction), students took notes and then answered a series of questions. Because students loved these "listening quizzes," they became a ritual. Later on, when the students begged for more short stories, I read them stories instead. Building a repertoire of stories that I could read in a few minutes, I created all kinds of questions from context vocabulary, to plot line sequence, to figures of speech in a 10-question quiz. The quiz was oral, which enhanced the listening aspect of the process. Working in quiet groups to generate the answers, they reinforced their note-taking skills and gained practice in all aspects of reading comprehension. The bonus: students were the ones to name these "Fun Friday."

I LIKE!!

Beloved Fun Friday Stories

"The Dinner Party" by Mona Gardner

"The Cage" by Martin Raim

"Appointment with Love" by S.I. Kishor

"The Wise Old Woman" retold by Yoshiko Uchida

"Matrimony Inn" by Lin Yutang

"The Sin of Madame Phloi" by Lilian Jackson Braun

"A Dip in the Poole" by Bill Bronzini

"Underwater Test" by Robert Zacks

"Two Were Left" by Hugh B. Cave

"The Story of an Hour" by Kate Chopin

"Charles" by Shirley Jackson

"Man with a Problem" by Donald Honig

"The Getaway" by John Savage

"The Lion Roared" by Virginia Eiseman

"The Gun" by Carol Ellis

"The Immortal Bard" by Isaac Asimov

"A Trick of the Trade" by Dorothy S. Pratt

Oh, the Irony of It All

There is nothing like the irony in a short story to snap middle school students out of their lethargy. They love surprises, and the literary surprises in some of the great classics are not only entertaining but also unleash their critical thinking skills. The ways you can support middle school students' learning about irony are

Make a connection: When some students struggle to understand the concept the first time the class encounters dramatic irony in a story, make a connection. Perhaps you remember struggling to understand it in middle school—let them know they are not alone; it is a tough concept. You might remember when you encountered irony in your own life and share the example.

Offer simple examples: "the police station was robbed last night"; "the firehouse burned down".

Ask students to share ironies of their own lives.

Little by little, watch the light bulbs turn on and irony can become one of the hallmarks of your literary explorations. Students can be enthralled at the inventiveness of these authors: Chekhov's irony of situation in "The Bet"; the wonderful twist at the end of deMaupassant's "The Necklace"; the hair raising ending to "The Interlopers."

U.o.S.

S-U-S-P-E-N-S-E!

Many middle school students still enjoy Halloween, so capitalize on their interest with a mini-unit of great suspense stories. In my experience, students loved the Halloween mania and begged for more Edgar Allan Poe, W.F. Harvey, and Daphne DuMaurier.

Focus the unit on writing style and imagery. Middle school students who find it very difficult to zero in on qualities that make each writer unique find it less troublesome with writers of this genre. Usually when analyzing a writer's use of imagery, students focus on what they can visualize, but suspense writers can show them the power of the other four senses.

Add a few stories from their past like "The Black Velvet Ribbon" (also known as "The Yellow Ribbon" or "The Red Ribbon") allowing students to reminisce about scary stories they love.

Talk about "suspension of disbelief" to address the ever-present group of students who try to apply reasoning and logic to stories that absolutely defy those qualities. Discussions about techniques in suspense stories can really focus students on story details and challenge their thinking in making connections to scientific reality.

Short Stories as Springboards for Writing

Teachers are inclined to assign literary essays and constructed responses as follow-ups to the study of short stories. These are important, especially in terms of analyzing literary elements like characterization, theme, setting, and conflict. Essays of comparison and contrast, persuasion, and cause and effect lend themselves well to writing about short stories. However, an overabundance of these in any language arts unit of study can be a real turn-off to adolescents and from a practical standpoint, overwhelming for the teacher in terms of timely grading and feedback. I found over the years that a judicious mixture of all kinds of writing formats kept all of us, students and teacher alike, enthusiastic about reading and writing responses. I also found that a teacher can evaluate a student's insight and skill in short pieces, and the teacher can give immediate feedback, which students crave and appreciate.

Short pieces could include:

- Memos and letters to me which immediately gave them a comfortable voice in which to express their views, make a judgment, or train a critical eye on some aspect of a story we were pondering

- Awards on their favorite story or author and write the rationale

- Explanation of the connection a poem or other very short story shared in common with the story we had studied

- A short scene (sometimes written individually, sometimes in a group) to end the story if the reader was left hanging at the end

Change Things Up

The key always in working with middle school students is to vary the task, to change things up. And this is an appropriate time to discuss the use of "I" in middle school writing. If teachers insist on removing the "I" point of view from every writing task, they might as well cut off their students' air supply because this is a time in their lives when students are exploring their world and their place in it. What I insisted on was that students had to be responsible to know when it was appropriate and when it was not. As more and more content area teachers foster writing in their own classrooms, language arts teachers have a bit more flexibility in the kinds of writing they can do with literature.

Examples of short responses.
A story like "The Bet" by Anton Chekhov allows for many short responses that give the teacher insight into students' thinking.

- Write a memo in which you react to the lawyer's decision.

- Explain which is most important to you: wisdom or riches.

- If you could have a conversation with the lawyer or the banker, describe what you would talk about.

- Explain whether this story has relevance in today's society.

Examples of prompts for students to respond to for "The Necklace" by Guy de Maupassant include

- Continue the conversation between Mathilde and Mme. Forestier where the story leaves off (maximum 10 lines).

- Mathilde ponders the "what if" she never lost the necklace. Explain the various ways she could have changed the direction of her life.

- What is your most prized possession and explain why is it so highly valuable to you.

- Discuss similarities between the banker in "The Bet" and Mathilde.

Stories for Analysis that Students Love

"The Bet" by Anton Chekhov

"The Necklace" by Guy de Maupassant

"The Falcon" by Giovanni Boccaccio

"The Interlopers" by Saki

"Dr. Heidegger's Experiment" by Nathaniel Hawthorne

"August Heat" by W.F. Harvey

"The Pit and the Pendulum" by Edgar Allan Poe

"The Cask of Amontillado" by Edgar Allan Poe

"The Birds" by Daphne DuMaurier

"The Monkey's Paw" by W.W. Jacobs

"The Boy Without a Name" by James Holding

"Hunger," "The Kitten" from *Black Boy* by Richard Wright

Story Dividends

Just a few short months into the school year, my students were hooked on English Language Arts. We had been reading and writing up a storm, but even more important, the tenor of the class was that found in seminars. I did not feel like the middle school teacher trying to control the class—the literature and writing topics were doing it for me. Students entered enthusiastic and eager to get to a story or resume a discussion or write a response. Analysis of the literature led to real connections to our lives revealing the maturity and wisdom of my students.

All of this work, the reading and the writing, went on during class. I did the narration of stories, and students never minded because they were in the spotlight more often than not. This allowed me to assign a book so that students were reading at home while our reading/writing workshop continued in class. All that we had worked on with stories would now be applicable to a more complex story—the class novel.

Chapter 4

"*Reading is a discount ticket to everywhere.*"
—Mary Schmich

The Novelty of Novels

When independent reading became more and more popular, I noticed that many English Language Arts teachers were abandoning the class novel. I am a great champion of the class novel for many reasons, but mainly because it enhances the building of the community of learners in a classroom and allows everyone to "be on the same page." The class novel, in a way, is a mini-text that provides all sorts of great opportunities for learning even beyond the important aspects of reading comprehension, vocabulary study, and analysis of literary elements. The novel that we all read gave us a well-spring of content from which to draw. We could take that book in any direction we wanted to go, and the opportunities for awakening student voice were limitless.

Many teachers get so frustrated assigning reading today because, quite frankly, many students just don't do it. Often these teachers will go chapter by chapter in class, but that is so punitive to the many students who do love to read and want to explore on their own and on their own schedules. It also can bog down the momentum of the book and rob students of their full engagement. I had my share of students who did not read the assigned class novel, but I was pretty successful in getting most students on board.

The Assignment

While I was doing other units in class, students would have two or three weeks to read the novel along with an "accountability assignment." I abandoned the old question/answer format and even the reading log because those are tedious for most students, and I did not want to take the joy out of these books. I also wanted them thinking more deeply as they read. Even though we were working on other things in class, students were always welcome to bring in their questions about the novel at the beginning of class each day. This served two purposes: obviously, I wanted to clear up their confusion, but also it generated interest for the procrastinators slow to start their reading. Once the book was due, we would have many reading and writing assignments, so I wanted the accountability piece to be something that helped students monitor their reading without being overwhelming. The following were accountability assignments I used; again to avoid predictability, I changed the assignment for each class novel.

- Because many of our class novels had only numbered chapters, students created chapter titles for each chapter with a brief explanation for each of their choices.

- Students chose to write a brief summary of each chapter, explain the major conflicts in each chapter, or sketch important scenes from each chapter and explain what the scene depicts. Often, I would use a mix of these, assigning one particular task for specified chapters.

- If a book had clearly defined characters, students would draw character "heads" (free-hand or computer-generated) and fill in the heads with physical attributes, characteristic sayings and actions, and personality descriptors.

- Readers who have trouble remembering what they read can place large sticky notes at the end of each chapter for recording character names, important plot lines, chief conflicts, as well as questions they have about the chapter amd difficult vocabulary. Checking the notes when the book is due, the teacher gains information related to future writing assignments for the novel.

- Students created an essential question for each chapter, then responded to it. Here are some examples:

  ◦ What does Character X's choice in Chapter 1 reveal about his character?

  ◦ In what ways are the family described in Chapter 8 dysfunctional, and how does that dysfunction affect the main character?

  ◦ In Chapter 4, how does the poem the main character recites reflect the conflicts he is working through?

- Students selected one or two important quotations from each chapter and explained their significance.

What's Old Can Be New Again

Using my old standby novels as texts, so to speak, I could do wonderful new things with them. Many of the teacher resource books that can be ordered with class novels are a fine place to start, but I still felt they fell short of what I wanted to accomplish. So essentially, I created my own novel modules that addressed higher standards and invited students to think more deeply, make connections to other readings and real life, and most importantly, discover the real "soul" of each book—teacher and students together. As the facilitator, my goal was to have each student gain new insights, broaden perspective, and explore new possibilities. The same happened for me as I researched content and themes, possible literary connections, and brainstormed innovative activities.

It was more a creative process than a proscribed method that led me to look at novels in new and more meaningful ways. Adaptable to any novel, the suggestions that follow show the infinite possibilities of the class novel. Combing through your own file cabinets can yield a treasure trove of materials long forgotten. There may well be great poems, short stories, and nonfiction pieces that offer new relevance to the class novels you plan to read.

The Planning Phase

As my focus shifted a bit away from more traditional approaches, I had a template for a generic process for each novel the students read. The key step was for me to determine what value I saw in the novel, why I was so passionate about having students read it, and what applications to my students' lives were inherent in the book.

Teacher's Planning Process

- List the important themes and issues of the novel.
- Examine what concepts, life lessons, aspects of the human condition the novel illumines.
- Decide what background material you and students have or can uncover that will generate interest about the novel.
- Find materials such as poems, non-fiction pieces, short stories, and news and magazine articles that

you may already have or you can find on the Internet
that connect to the novel's themes/issues.

- Plan in-class activities for the novel unit.
- Decide what kinds of writing you want to
  incorporate as well as possible projects.

Three Examples of Whole Class Novels

The following three novels were mainstays of my classroom for
years. What they have in common is that I love them as a reader
first, and they speak to middle school students. Then as the teacher,
I believed in their value for my students. I share some thoughts
about each, as well as ideas for activities, writing springboards,
and other literary connections. You may have your favorites, and
that is the point—teach what you love—I am offering these more as
models of the whole class novel experience.

1. *Stuck in Neutral* by Terry Trueman

The perfect class novel to begin the school year, this book is highly
"readable" in a fairly short space of time for all levels of students.
Yet it raises the truly big questions, presents students with critical
thinking dilemmas, and stimulates dialogue about many topics.
Although this novel lends itself to many different approaches, I
share here those that really "awakened" my students.

Activities

Read aloud the first few chapters. They are short but will arouse
student interest immediately. Shawn McDaniel, the main character,
literally "hits them over the head" from the start, and students get

sucked in right away. Reading the rest as homework, students will finish the book in a week to 10 days. Have students create titles for each chapter while you use classroom time for activities related to the novel.

- After students hear Chapter One read aloud, they write a letter to the teacher explaining how their lives are a "good news-bad news" joke. This is an opportunity for students to find their voice in their writing, really open their hearts, and reveal themselves as human beings.

- Groups come up with their definitions of "disability." They discuss real people they know with disabilities. Despite their reputation for lacking in compassion, adolescents are capable of deep insights about real people with disabilities.

- Using a computer lab or laptops, students research cerebral palsy and report their findings to the class. During discussion, students add only new bits of information to what other students have already reported.

- On YouTube, stream or access clips on disabilities, especially cerebral palsy. Provide articles, especially from the point of view of parents of disabled children to set the stage for discussions about the McDaniel family.

- The book's powerful ending will have students excited and agitated as they discuss it. Have students form groups based on their similar beliefs in the outcome for Shawn. Groups must trace evidence in the book to support their point of view.

- After students discuss whether one man can decide the fate of his disabled son, present students with some real life moral dilemmas. Internet searches of moral dilemmas will yield many examples to spark phenomenal discussions. Another option is for students to create their own moral dilemmas.

- If the back cover of the students' books has a quote (such as the ALA Booklist's "*Stuck in Neutral* is an intense reading experience."), ask students to improve on capturing the power of the novel in their own quotation. This simple exercise forces them to review and synthesize content and use their creative juices. The class can choose the best of the best from all classes to be the quotes of the week during the novel study.

Essential Questions

Ask students why they think the novel was chosen for the class to read. After they jot down the possible reasons, students then write the important questions the novel forces the reader to think about. Students will cite the obvious reasons—disabilities, family conflicts, and euthanasia. Some will even notice Terry Trueman's writing style and the narrative framework as very different from the usual. Others will notice differences of mothers and fathers in childrearing. Although students may empathize with a disabled person, many will have immense difficulty comprehending the lack of ability to communicate and see it as the ultimate disability. These are some of the essential questions resulting from our discussions.

- Is it possible for a man to be both good and bad?
- Can a family member ever "divorce" another member of that family?
- Is the kind of life described in the novel a life worth living?
- Is schooling valuable for those considered "uneducable"?
- How do we get beyond the outside veneers of people to reveal who they really are inside?

Literary Elements

Writers's style. Middle school students have a difficult time analyzing a writer's style, and this book can foster great discussion on how writers approach their subjects. Terry Trueman, through the character Shawn, uses an almost stream-of-consciousness narration style. A great analytical exercise is for students to figure out how else the author could have treated his subject. Students discover themselves that the subject of severe cerebral palsy could have been approached in myriad ways, but the author of this novel chose his unique approach.

Character analysis. Students examine the differences in the family members, and how each might have told the story from his or her point of view. The character of Shawn also illumines other themes in the book besides his disability and euthanasia such as the effects of divorce on the family, the media, parenting, and our schools.

Literary Connections

"Teen's Story is TALL Tale," *Current Science*, Volume 94, Issue 9, and www.thetallestman.com/brendenadams.htm. This wonderful non-fiction piece extends the discussion of disabilities. It is the story of a teen who copes with a genetic disability that causes day-to-day challenges for him. Comparing Shawn McDaniel and Brenden in terms of their struggles elicits mature insight and wisdom from students.

"Helen Keller's Long Lost Child" by Ruth Harrigan. Students love this poem because it is relevant to their own lives as well as connected to their reading of *Stuck in Neutral*. Shawn and the man and the girl in the poem are bound by loneliness and isolation, but Shawn's hope for "being known" is exemplified as a possibility in the poem when the girl "lays a hand" on the man's "gnarled one."

"Slightly Disabled, Not Helpless or Dumb," *The New York Times,* by Jennifer Bartlett. Students can see the parallels between Shawn and Jennifer, especially the way they "talk" about their cerebral palsy. The article shows the degrees of cerebral palsy—what Jennifer was able to accomplish in her life, what Shawn was not.

MyChild at CerebralPalsy.org is a treasure trove of information and inspiration on many facets of the subject that can be used for making connections to the novel.

Writing Springboards

I made it a practice in my class to really mix up the kinds of writing tasks I gave my students. Adolescents will balk at anything repetitive and predictable. Though content area teachers refrain from having students use "I" and inject personal opinion into more formal work, I tried in English Language Arts to be flexible enough to encourage both. The key, as I cautioned students, was to know when their less formal voice was appropriate to the task, and when it was not.

Personal Topics

- Shawn has a gift of remembering everything he hears. Explain what gift you would want.

- Shawn's senses are keen. Of the five senses, explain which is most valuable to you.

- Describe how you felt when the family pet had to be euthanized or how a friend or family member felt (for those students who cannot relate, change to Imagine how you would feel...)

- Explain your perceptions of the treatment of the physically and developmentally disabled in our society.

- Give a short introduction to the story from another character's point of view.

- Using Shawn's stream of consciousness approach, write about a moment, a day, or a time in your life.

- Write the next scene after the story ends.

- We are taught that fighting is wrong. Can you defend on any moral ground what Paul does to the bullies?

Formal Topics

- Explain whether you believe Shawn's life is a life worth living. Give evidence from the novel for support.

- The "uneducable" should receive an education. Defend or refute this statement.

- Explain whether Shawn's father is a good man, bad man, or a combination of the two.

- Explain which character in the novel experiences the most profound conflicts.

- Consider and explain the various circumstances in which a person has a "right-to-die."

- It is ironic that the "retard" is incredibly intelligent and intuitive. Discuss other examples of irony in the novel.

- What is your definition of "quality of life"? Explain whether or not Shawn has it.

2. *The Outsiders* by S.E. Hinton

No matter how many times I taught this book, I loved it. A great novel for character and conflict study, it is also a manifesto on teen-hood (pardon the pun), as relevant today as it was when Susan

Eloise Hinton wrote it as a 16-year-old. There are many universal truths revealed in this book, and I believe Hinton "wrote the book" on all it means to be a teen. The following suggestions helped my students discover profound insights.

Activities

Most often the focus of the book is centered on the conflicts between the Greasers and the Socs and what makes Ponyboy different from the rest of the gang. But to leave it at that is a grave injustice. The following are some means of exploring the novel to uncover deeper analysis, and to get students on to a whole other journey, one in which their voices are dominant over the teacher's.

- When students express much sadness about the novel's ending, capitalize on their emotional reactions. Students can write their emotional reactions on a clipboard (with or without names) with the understanding that the teacher will share them and the class will discuss them.

- Students create book quotations to replace the ones on the back of their paperbacks. Express confidence that their quotations about the book would be more inspiring than the ones on the inside cover and on the back of their books. Aim for them to capture the essence of their emotional reactions as well synthesize their thoughts. The class can vote on the best one from each class, narrow those down to one, which can be on the board for the duration of the novel unit.

- This activity probes the deeper meaning of the book. First pose the question: "What are the important themes and issues in the novel?" Most students will say "the in vs. out crowd" or "gangs. " Next, students do "an open book." In groups, they jot down words, phrases, issues, lessons, character names, conflicts—anything and everything that comes to mind about the novel. Then, as you circulate through the room, prod and probe about what their jottings mean. This should yield a whole new layer of themes and issues and a greater awareness in students of just what a book can offer readers:

- How our ideas about family can be redefined
- How heroes come in many forms
- How life is full of "what ifs"
- How our environment shapes who we become
- How we often do not get to see beneath the veneers of people.

• Before starting your lesson plans, ask students to consider the following scenario: if you were the teacher planning activities for *The Outsiders* what would they be? Example suggestions from students are

- Work with the poem "Nothing Gold Can Stay"
- Have a debate between the Greasers and the Socs
- Do sketches of pivotal scenes
- Act out scenes

Answering this simple question invests students in ownership and commitment to the work. I absolutely did use the students' suggestions from analyzing "Nothing Gold Can Stay," then had students write their own poems capturing similar themes. They would also write skits and act them out, organize the Great Debate, and prepare talking points for the Greasers and the Socs.

Essential Questions

By creating essential questions about *The Outsiders,* students uncover the heart of the matter, engage in reflection, and bring their own experiences to the table to make sense of what they have read. Accustomed to finding the right answer, students often do not consider that there are many possible answers. Likewise, they are accustomed to specific, narrow questions rather than "big idea" questions. If we want to awaken middle grades students' minds as well as their voices, they must learn how to learn, which involves pondering, assessing, evaluating, relating, and inquiring. Over the years these were the types of questions my students "grew into."

Why does *The Outsiders* have such staying power after all these years in terms of popularity and relevance?

How does this coming of age novel realistically mirror the road to maturity?

Does all that is "gold" inevitably lose its luster?

How many layers of meaning are there to the word "outsider"?

Does the traditional nuclear family foster the best chances of success for the children?

Literary Elements

Students are usually pros at examining character, plot, and conflict, and the effects of setting, especially in such graphic texts as *The Outsiders.* However, I think a bit of time spent on irony is worth the effort: authors rely on the reader to uncover the hidden meanings or discern unexpected outcomes. Analyzing dramatic or situational irony requires a bit of mental gymnastics, and students feel rewarded, and yes, intelligent, when they figure things out.

Have students list all the examples of irony in the book, and once they get started, not only will they have fun, but also they will think deeply. Students may list these examples of irony: this book is actually Pony's composition for class; the Socs have a human side; the cold, hard exterior of Dallas conceals his love for Johnny; Johnny is branded a murderer when he becomes a hero; the rumble is a heralded event; the realization that fighting does not solve anything; Darry was a Soc; the Dally "bluff"; Johnny wanting to live after he wanted to die; Pony's missing curfew leading to a chain of tragic events.

Literary Connections

"Richard Cory" by Edwin Arlington Robinson. Great parallels to *The Outsiders*. Students associate Richard Cory with the Socs and the people on the pavement with the Greasers. Bob and Richard Cory are similar in that they seem to have everything, but below the surface, they are not happy. Themes of stereotyping, making judgments, envy of others. A great discussion of the possibilities of why Richard ends his life.

"On the Bridge" by Todd Strasser. Character connections between Seth and Adam and Pony and the rest of the gang. Themes of staying true to oneself, consequence of action, symbols of coolness. Students get excited about the ramifications of peer pressure and making bad choices.

"The Uncertain Gang Member" from "One in 8 Million" *The New York Times*. Joshua Febres is a product of his environment, a neighborhood in the Bronx where Crips rule. Wonderful connections to the members of the Greasers, especially Ponyboy, in that all have to weigh doing "the right thing and avoid doing the wrong thing."

The Freedom Writers Diary with Erin Gruwell. Devote as much time as you can spare to this work that allows myriad opportunities for connections and parallels to *The Outsiders* but also gives rise to student voice through discussion and writing their own diary entries. The Freedom Writers inspire middle school students with their descriptions of racism, hatred, and pain. Choose excerpts that reflect gang mentality, self-preservation, and living on the wrong side of the tracks.

"The Accident" from *North Toward Home* by Willie Morris. I used this very short piece to have students evaluate whether the men on the train equate to the Socs in terms of their indifference or something more is going on. It makes for a very interesting discussion. Also, the scene depicted in the story is a "small tableau to violence and death in the city."

Writing Springboards

Personal Topics

- Use the opening "When I stepped out…I had only two things on my mind…" to explain what is on your mind.

- Just as S.E. Hinton brings her characters alive on paper, do the same by describing someone you know in depth.

- If Ponyboy had not overslept in the vacant lot, many events might not have occurred. Recall and describe a big "what if" in your own life.

- What does it take to be considered a hero in your eyes?

- What do you think happens to the remaining gang members when the novel ends?

- Write a short poem by finishing "Gold is…"

- Write a diary entry about an experience you had that involved racism, intolerance, or bullying.

Formal Topics

- Explain why this novel endures in popularity almost 50 years after it was first published.

- Explain which character endures the greatest conflicts in the novel.

- Explore the meanings behind Johnny's last words, "Stay gold, Ponyboy, stay gold."

- Outline the significant themes of *The Outsiders*, and explain which prevails in terms of greatest importance.

- Many say that this novel shows the reader that we are "all the same." Explain whether you agree or disagree with this statement.

- Explain whether you agree or disagree with the statement "Nothing Gold Can Stay."

- Johnny tells Ponyboy that "fighting is useless." Explain whether or not there are times in life when fighting is necessary.

3. *The Pigman* by Paul Zindel

Over the years, I have read hundreds of books of fiction geared toward adolescents, and this remains one of my top picks because of its humor and I can relate well to John and Lorraine, the misfits. As I said, the more passionate I was about a book, the more justice I could do to the teaching of it. I also tended to do this book in the spring, as we were heading toward the finish line of the school year. *The Pigman* offered endless opportunities for more lighthearted fare, which we often needed after spring break.

Activities

Introducing this book by reading the first few chapters out loud helps to get students used to the narrative technique of John and Lorraine taking turns telling the story, and in the process, revealing so much about themselves. Both characters make it readily apparent that their lives and problems mirror those of students. Students can immediately discuss Zindel's characterization techniques.

- Have students complete "Open Minds" when the book is due. Students fill their computer-generated or drawn heads with descriptive words and phrases that capture personality and physical traits, as well as sayings and actions the characters are known for in the novel. This becomes a natural lead-in to initial class discussions.

- Groups of students create a list of important themes in the novel. Likely student answers include: school issues, dysfunctional families, friendship, teen vices, death, alienation, values, and coming of age. Assign each group one of those themes and have them explain how Zindel treats that theme in the novel. Students can find themes, illustrations, key passages or lines from the book to demonstrate their specific theme. Each group reports to the class.

- Mr. Pignati's "Assassin Game" is a great springboard for discussion about a person's values. Have students rate persons from most to least responsible for the wife's death in the game. This is a wonderful deep thinking exercise.

(Most students believe the wife bears responsibility for her own demise because it was her choice to go off with the lover, a most interesting flip in that adolescents will often blame others rather than take onus for their own actions.) They would take exception to my choice, the assassin, because they felt it was a paid job, but my values tell me it is never moral to take another's life. Note that this little game leads to a heavy duty discussion about belief systems beyond the playful key that Mr. P shares with John and Lorraine about what their choices reveal about them. To extend the learning, have student groups create their own scenarios modeled after the "Assassin Game," another challenging exercise requiring brain power and creativity.

- Pose the question, "What do you think Mr. Pignati would have thought about the Internet?" In my classes, this allowed me to bring in all those amazing little-known facts, brain teasers, things that make you go "Hmmm...," silly questions that we all get via e-mail. Students loved these, and always wanted to bring in their own examples. Because all three characters love far-fetched stories and weird accounts, I would also share some Urban Legends dedicating them to John, Lorraine, and Mr. Pignati.

Essential Questions

It is easy to get sidelined by Zindel's use of humor and forget that this fun novel raises some very serious questions. Students are very much clued in, though, to the issues that are raised, especially because they can relate to the conflicts and dysfunction. The following questions are the result of teacher/student collaboration.

- Where is the dividing line between immaturity and maturity?

- How many forms can friendship take?

- Are parents responsible for their children's irresponsible behavior?

- What are some causes of alienation?

- When is the Generation Gap not a "gap"?

Literary Elements

This book is a classic for teaching characterization techniques. All its characters provide fertile ground for exploring hundreds of character traits. In addition, having John and Lorraine take turns narrating chapters allows them to clue the reader in to different dimensions of each other as well as how they perceive the other characters in the book. This book also offers a unique opportunity to examine how very minor characters in a novel can be extraordinarily important as catalysts for plot changes and dramatic conflict. Focusing on Dennis and Norton with students can illuminate this point. Spend a bit of time discussing Zindel's use of pictures, images, and diagrams in a book geared for adolescents, again part of the author's style and his intent to break up the reading for those easily distracted and in keeping with the light-hearted nature of the book.

Literary Connections

"Birthday Party" by Katharine Brush. Students write a letter to the man in the story from Mr. Pignati's point of view requiring them to really get into the Pigman's mindset and write from his values and beliefs about marriage. My own students would often reflect their empathy with the woman in the story as they admonished the man for his treatment of his wife.

"The Little Boy and the Old Man" by Shel Silverstein. This little nugget of a poem challenges students to see the relationship between Mr. Pignati and John and Lorraine in terms of how much they all have in common. It underscores the alienation theme of the novel: Mr. Pignati and the old man isolated and alone, John and Lorraine, kind of misfits and misunderstood by parents.

"Mirror" by Sylvia Plath. Talk about the woman in the poem, but then discuss ways the Pigman (students will view him as an old man although he is 58 in the novel) clung to youthful endeavors trying to fill the void of his wife's death. Hold a class discussion about aging in our society, for both men and women.

Writing Springboards

If you have time, give students all of these topics. Students love this activity, and the topics will help students really relate their own experiences to the greater human condition—which is the beauty of the novel—students looking at their lives in a context that is new to them.

Personal Topics

- The best way to describe my best friend is…
- My parents just don't seem to understand…
- I'm known for…
- The best prank I ever pulled…
- I know a kid just like Norton…
- My (mother, father) has such a bad habit…
- My favorite hangout…
- My day at school is…

- I just love going to…

- I know someone like Mr. Pignati…

- If only I had not…

- The best way to describe my family is…

- The strangest food I ever ate…

Formal Topics

- Describe John and Lorraine when you "meet" them at the beginning of the novel. In what ways have they changed as the novel ends?

- Decide whether you would defend or prosecute John and Lorraine for the death of Mr. Pignati. Write your arguments as you would present them in court.

- Lorraine says, "Maybe there are some lies you should never admit to." Do you agree or disagree? Explain your position.

- Paul Zindel said that the following must be ingredients of a young adult book: romance, honesty, mischief, action, and suspense. Explain whether or not each of these five elements is evident in *The Pigman* using illustrations from the novel for support.

- Explain the meaning of the following quotation at the end of the novel. "Baboons. Baboons. They build their own cages, we could almost hear the Pigman whisper, as he took his children with him."

- If you have read *The Outsiders* as a class: In a well-developed extended response, explain why *The Pigman* could be retitled *The Outsiders*.

- In what ways do individuals become alienated from society? Illustrate examples you have witnessed in your own experience.

- Describe the various forms of friendship in our lives other than the "best friend relationship" you are so familiar with.

Other Possibilities

There are so many amazing titles in the young adult novel genre! I spent year after year forgoing my own reading in pursuit of the best novels for my students. Though many fit the bill, I always had to narrow my choices due to important factors.

- Would I get parent complaints?
- Did the book speak to one gender over another?
- Was it readable for a wide variety of reading levels heterogeneously grouped?
- Did it meet my number one requirement, awakening the middle school voice?

My searches were never in vain; my students appreciated my ability to make recommendations based on their interests, reading abilities, and their liberal or conservative parents. I offer here a mere sampling of other title suggestions for the class novel. They have a great deal in common:

- controversial topics and teenage issues
- coming-of-age themes
- moral dilemmas and conflicts
- real-life/historical connections

My students readily identified with the main characters, were able to make connections to prior reading, especially *The Outsiders* and *The Pigman*, and were moved by and vocal about each in myriad ways. From a teacher standpoint, each lends itself beautifully to

"The Planning Process" I have outlined. I imagine all teachers have their favorite novels to infect students with whatever makes them favorites and look at them from all angles, especially those that foster analysis, evaluation, and making judgments. Here is my short list:

Driver's Ed by Caroline B. Cooney

Heat by Mike Lupica

Nothing but the Truth by Avi

Scorpions by Walter Dean Myers

Tangerine by Edward Bloor

The Cage by Ruth Minsky Sender

The Giver by Lois Lowry

The River by Gary Paulsen

The Trouble with Lemons by Daniel Hayes

The Wave by Todd Strasser

Chapter 5

"We dance around the ring and suppose,
but the secret sits in the middle and knows."
—Robert Frost

Midterms? Let's Get Creative

Midterms were not a requirement in the school in which I
taught, so some teachers gave them and some did not. I was
always conflicted about giving mid-year exams because as an
English Language Arts teacher, I had myriad ways of assessing
students, from various writing assignments and essays to
projects. I periodically assessed students' growth by evaluating
their cumulative writing folders. I had learned early on to collect
all their written work because students were not dependable in
completing this task, and it is critically important for students to
look at past work and evaluate their progress.

Mid-Year Test

I first used a comprehensive essay test to provide a look at what
students had done and evaluate their learning. It required students
to synthesize material, make connections between literary pieces,
and evaluate and make judgments about all the pieces they had
read. However, that approach did not fulfill what I really wanted

to get out of this middle-of-the-year pause. I knew I wanted students discussing this large body of literature, I wanted them collaborating on how they were affected by these authors and their works, and I wanted them to take ownership of these works and use them in a creative way. And so the Mid-Year Literary Project was conceived.

The Mid-Year Literary Project

The project is a result of constant tweaking and upgrading to address issues with student work and with grading procedures, which I simplified by using task-specific rubrics. You can search the Internet for task-specific rubrics for videos, scrapbooks—you name it. I gave students these tips:

Movie guidelines: no foul language, no dangerous filming locations, teacher views for final approval, consider getting parent approval.

Group work decision: decide whether the exciting, extremely productive, and terrific learning experiences for all the students involved is worth the logistics of getting the group together, relying on a particular person for an integral piece of the project, or procrastination.

Study the exemplars and sub-par examples: examine former student projects and determine what makes the difference between projects on the continuum from great to sub-par.

The Assignment: Mid-Year Literary Project

This is an opportunity to stop and reflect on all the wonderful literature we have read so far, and at the same time, showcase your

talents. You can work individually, with a partner, or in a group—
you decide; just remember the pitfalls of relying on others if that
has been a problem for you in the past! Perhaps you would like to
produce a film, do an art project, make an oral presentation, write a
sequel, or use technology in some unique, creative way. You choose
the literary work(s) as a springboard, you decide the format that is
compatible with your talents, and then let the creative juices flow.
We will brainstorm ideas in class, but you are the master of this
project. You do need my approval for all projects.

If you do a film based on our reading of novels or short stories, you
must do more than re-film scenes, perhaps reworking the story in
some fashion, adding scenes that might have happened; in other
words, use the literature as a departure point for innovative work.

Examples

- Host a talk show with characters from a story or
  novel. Plan the questions and responses.

- Create a portfolio of sketches depicting key
  scenes from a variety of stories we read.

- Write a sequel to one of the many stories that left us "hanging"
  or write what happens next after one of our novels leaves off.

- Design a scrapbook that showcases your favorite stories/books.

- Create a poetry book—write poems reflecting themes,
  conflicts, characters from a novel or stories we read.

Spark Enthusiasm

When passing out the assignment sheet, give students a list of all
the short stories and novels they have read the first half of the year

to help them remember the characters and storylines and start their thinking about which works they want to showcase. At this point a major goal of the project is underway; the works they have read are not a list of isolated works on a curriculum sheet, but a body of literature that can spark conversation, fresh ideas, and a whole new purpose.

Troubleshooting

Some nuts-and-bolts directives that made managing the project much easier:

- No giant-size posters or paper that would take up too much space
- No cumbersome scrapbooks; use notebook-size
- All films have to be on a DVD—no wires hanging from video cameras requiring special hookups
- Art portfolios have to be on standard paper or a sketch pad

In fact a guideline sheet for easy reference gets this all out on the table beforehand and makes for a much smoother project and far fewer hurt feelings.

Guidelines for Mid-Year Literary Project

The most important thing to remember is to use the novels and short stories as springboards for ideas, not simply retelling the plot lines. The purpose of the project is to showcase your originality and creativity.

- All written projects should be double-spaced, proofread, and edited for proper use of dialogue, spelling, capitalization, and punctuation.

- Oral presentations of skits, readings, etc., if not filmed, will be performed in class.

- Scrapbooks and poetry books should be of manageable size and properly bound.

- Technology projects should reflect evidence of planning and organization, appropriate language and subject matter, safe and orderly conditions "on location," and good, sound judgment.

Celebrate

I recommend about three weeks to complete the Mid-Year Literary Project. On the due date, celebrate the students' ingenuity and creativity. From skits, to art work, to poetry books, to song writing, the project yields more educational intangibles than the products themselves. If the vision for a middle school classroom is one that includes reveling in successes, eye-opening discovery, collaborating about material, participation of all stakeholders, pure, rapt attention—then the Mid-Year Literary Project fulfills the mission.

Chapter 6

"What is wonderful about great literature is that it transforms the man who reads it towards the condition of the man who wrote it."

—E. M. Forster

Author Seminar

One of the maladies of a middle school literature curriculum can be the slapdash approach to authors, titles, genres, and themes. I liken it to dabbling in "this or that," very superficially without depth. The whole year's offerings can seem like samples on a smorgasbord without students really savoring anything in particular. So years ago I decided to have students experience a short story writer and a number of his works. I chose William Sydney Porter, O. Henry, because I love irony, and what I love, I tend to teach well. However, I think the works of H. H. Munro better known as Saki, or Edgar Allan Poe would be wonderful choices as well. My major goal was to have students delve into the writer's style, and that is so difficult to do when you expose them to one or even two works. I also used the unit as an opportunity to foster a bit of creative writing, which seems to be disappearing in middle school, to make room for standardized testing writing formats.

Why O. Henry?

- The stories are readable for a wide audience of diverse tastes that informs the middle school classroom.

- O. Henry's characters deepen students' understanding of the human condition, and he poses conflicts and dilemmas that tap adolescents' moral imagination.

- Students learn a great deal about themselves as well as humanity when they react to an O. Henry story, for example the consequences of decisions or perhaps, the moral dilemmas real people face every day.

- The world of O. Henry quite simply is entertaining and lots of fun, the surest way to awaken the middle school voice.

Beginning the Unit

I began this course of study with background on "The Gift of the Magi." When I gave students the plot summary, many recognized the story because they had seen it in its many guises on television and cartoons. They loved the ironic twist, and that was the only spark necessary to get them interested in William Sydney Porter. Often, I would have the students research interesting facts about him as well as his stories. Middle school students love a good background story on an author, and William Sydney Porter, the theories behind his pen name, and his jack-of-all-trades work history fit the bill. It was also great fun to give background on life at the turn of the twentieth century from life expectancy to salaries to costs of food.

Stories

Once students heard one story, they would rush in each day asking what O. Henry story we would be doing next. I tried to read as many stories as time would allow from the following list.

"After Twenty Years"

"A Retrieved Reformation"

"The Cop and the Anthem"

"The Last Leaf"

"The Love Powder"

"The Ransom of Red Chief"

"Two Thanksgiving Day Gentlemen"

Literary Elements

As in any short story unit, we would discuss the literary elements of plot, characterization, setting, and theme upon completion of each story. However, the exciting work began when we had read a few stories: students began to draw parallels, make connections, and find similarities and differences. These stories provided such fertile ground for discussion and group collaboration as well as written work of all kinds.

Essential Questions

The following essential questions can serve as topics for group seminar discussions and reporting out or writing prompts.

- Critics say that O. Henry is the master of the ironic twist. Explain what they mean in terms of the stories you have read by O. Henry.

- How would you describe O. Henry's writing style to someone who has never read his stories? One approach to answering this question might be to consider what the stories have in common.

- So many of O. Henry's characters are larger than life and thus, memorable. Describe the character you believe to be "unforgettable," and explain how O. Henry makes this happen.

- Which O. Henry character do you believe faces the most difficult decision? On what basis do you justify your choice?

- In what ways do the life and times of William Sydney Porter himself make their way into his stories?

Using Quotations as Springboards

Another wonderful approach is to give students quotations that can be great springboards for discussion or, again, written responses. One of my favorites is by the author himself: "Life is made up of sobs, sniffles and smiles, with sniffles predominating." Not only do his words reflect the man students come to "know" but compel them to go back into the stories and evaluate and make judgments about characters, conflicts, and themes.

- "Conscientious people are apt to see their duty in that which is the most painful course."
  —George Eliot

- "Man is a being with free will; therefore, each man is potentially good or evil, and it's up to him and only him (through his reasoning mind) to decide which he wants to be."
  —Ayn Rand

- "What seems to us as bitter trials are often blessings in disguise."
  —Oscar Wilde

- "Irony is jesting behind hidden gravity."
  —John Weiss

- "Nothing is to be preferred before justice."
  —Socrates

- "We improve ourselves by victories over ourselves. There must be contest, and we must win."
  —Edward Gibbon

These are just samples of quotations that can inform discussion or writing topics. Another wonderful exercise is to have the students themselves search for quotations that are applicable to their study of O. Henry and his works.

Have *Students* Make Comparisons

Making comparisons is a skill easily addressed in this unit, but teachers tend to offer up the comparisons (example: Jimmy Wells and Ben Price) and then ask students to justify them. I think it is far better to have students uncover the comparisons themselves. My experience shows that, given time for collaboration, students find that while Silky Bob and Jimmy Valentine begin in similar circumstances, their paths widely diverge. They see the commonalities of qualities and choices of Berman, Ralph Spencer, and the Old Gentleman. They unearth O. Henry's use of wit and playfulness in the telling of "The Cop and the Anthem" and "Two Thanksgiving Day Gentlemen." Students easily identify a prevailing theme of good vs. evil in these stories, but what is most exciting is to listen to them evaluate the degree to which each character exhibits them. For example, most students do not see Micky Shack as problematic as Silky Bob, and they often give Soapy a pass despite the crimes he commits while trying to gain entrance to jail. They can be pretty tough on Joanna when she is losing hope and even tougher on Jimmy Wells because he "ratted out" his friend, a real problem with many adolescents.

Whatever your students unearth during this in-depth study of O. Henry's works, there are sure to be lively discussions, excited exploration, and some insightful writing going on. I always felt that this "author seminar" was a mirror into what all education should be about.

Films

View a few films of O. Henry's stories, especially "The Cop and the Anthem" and "After Twenty Years." Students love to point out details that differ in the filmed versus written version, a wonderful stretch of the brain. Then give students some fun writing exercises as an extension to all the analysis, evaluation, and making judgments that came out of the discussion and writing based on the written story. These are just a few of them.

- Find story starter ideas on the Internet, and have students, alone or in small groups, write a tight, one-page story (put a limit on length because middle school students can get lost in their own stories) that has an ironic twist at the end in the manner of O. Henry. Caution them against, "I woke up and it was all a dream!"

- Have students capture the conversation, in dialogue, that they would have with their favorite or least favorite O. Henry character.

- Have students write a memo to O. Henry capturing their observations about his stories in general or a specific character, plot line, irony, or situation they found interesting or maybe even taking the author to task on something they took issue with.

- Have students write the next scene after the surprise twist.

Chapter 7

"If we value independence, if we are disturbed by the growing conformity of knowledge, of values, of attitudes, which our present system induces, then we may wish to set up conditions of learning which make for uniqueness, for self-direction, and for self-initiated learning."

—Carl Rogers

Let's Get Published!

Many years ago my middle school required teachers to do some kind of research project. Students would complain that doing so many reports was boring and repetitive. For example, they might have chosen a mathematician from a list and researched his/her life and contributions. In health class they would research the causes, symptoms, and treatment of a disease. There was also much inconsistency in the required formats and the teaching of research skills. Later there would be attempts at interdisciplinary projects, but at least among my colleagues, planning got bogged down on how the "grade would count" and who was going to read what part of the project. My students continued to complain, and I would try to create something that I felt was more relevant to them—author projects, historical novel projects, and career projects. My students were not impressed.

A New Idea

Almost 25 years ago, a workshop presented by Shoreham-Wading River School District on an interdisciplinary project called The

Inquiry Project planted the seed of a new idea. Showcasing research methods, the project encouraged the rhetorical modes of writing and student creativity, and though I could not sell the project as an interdisciplinary one back at my own school due to the same old hangups, a colleague and I tweaked the project for our needs. Essentially, students chose a topic and then mapped out ways their subject related to the courses they were taking: social studies, math, science, health, etc. After completing their research, they used different writing modes, perhaps a narrative or poetry or question/answer interview to include in their final product—a bound portfolio of interdisciplinary connections and a visual representation that applied to the topic, perhaps a diagram or graph or artistic representation. Subject area teachers acted as mentors of their fields. For example, if a student had chosen a sport, the social studies teacher might guide the student in researching the long history behind that sport.

And so it went for some years. Students enjoyed the project but as often happens if you give middle school students new paths to explore, they often become inventors of something bigger and better. Even before technology had taken its hold, students were enthusiastically asking if they could "go crazy" on their cover designs. They wanted to add touches to the written pages with drawings or sketches. They asked if they could go beyond the required number of pages they were supposed to write. As they researched, they began to see new possibilities for their written work.

I share with you the magazine project as I assigned it for my English Language Arts class after years of tweaking and re-inventing. When I presented the project in professional workshops, I encouraged teachers to think in terms of the interdisciplinary approach if they were so inclined. I also encouraged them to tweak what needed tweaking for their own subject area needs or use it as a springboard for other ideas. Nothing has to be set in stone in terms of requirements. A teacher's vision and creativity are the only requisites. Then the students do the rest. They love to adorn each page with beautiful graphics, change fonts and colors to suit their article topics, and design covers that are incredibly professional looking. They have fun "hamming up" their about-the-editor pages and really rise to the occasion writing interesting, informative, insightful articles. The feedback from parents was overwhelmingly positive. Most said they had never seen their children work as hard on any school project—ever!

A Word or Two About Group Work

I think the project lends itself to students working with a partner or at most, in threes. For groups, the requirements for numbers of articles and visuals, double or triple, and groups need more variety in sources and writing modes. Whatever the project, I always cautioned my students about group work in terms of accountability, time constraints, and logistics. For the first time out, I would recommend each student working alone, then as with other aspects of the project, the teacher has flexibility to make modifications and changes.

Magazine Project

You are going to publish a magazine! This project combines research, writing, technology, and graphic design skills through self-directed learning about a topic you always wanted to know more about. Throughout the project, remember that your final product will be the facsimile of a real magazine. A presentation binder with plastic sleeves will showcase your project the best.

Your publication will contain the following:

- A cover
- An about-the-editor page
- Table of contents
- 6 articles minimum—you are free to do more!
- 1 visual minimum—you can have others.
- Works Cited page (Minimum of 6 sources, 1 encyclopedia maximum)

very similar to mine !! (handwritten margin note)

The Process

- Choose a topic you really want to learn more about.
- Choose at least 4 different writing modes and 1 visual mode from the "menu" below. The purpose of this is to mirror real magazine articles; you use the research as background for the type of articles you want to write.
- Prepare a Works Cited page using MLA format.
- Be sure to use citations for "borrowed" information as outlined in Library class.

Writing Modes: Description, Narration, Explanation, Persuasion, Comparison/Contrast, Cause/Effect, Report, News Article, Glossary, Editorial, Poetry, Fact Sheet, Interview, Question & Answer, Quiz.

revise to include more

Visual Modes: Diagram, Drawing, Illustration, Graph, Chart, Spread Sheet, Original Photography, Collage, Film Clip, Word Search, Time Line

Sample Topic: A golf magazine might include the following articles: a persuasive essay on the health benefits of the game; a fact sheet on the history of the game; a glossary of golf terms; an analysis of scoring and yardage; poetry on the beauty of the golfing environment; an interview with someone you know who plays the game; a comparison of golf fashion "then and now." Your visual might be a graph showing the results of a survey you took on how many students play golf seriously, how many have tried it, and how many have no interest.

Because I wanted to make the actual assignment sheet one page for easy reference, I gave additional information in class on writing modes and visuals, and I helped students brainstorm ideas for topics that might be of interest to them. Looking at projects from former students acted as springboards for their own imaginations.

The Process

I gave students 4-5 weeks to complete the project. Before launching into the project, students looked at magazines and former students' projects. Though many students happily worked independently and budgeted their time appropriately, more and more students needed reminders of where they needed to be on the project timeline to make their deadlines. Week by week I gave them guidelines as to where they should be in the process.

> **Week 1.** Students chose topics. Research began in
> the school library with our library media specialist

teaching mini-lessons on Works Cited form and embedded citations, giving students a template so that they could keep track of source information. Students had a few class periods to start research so they could firm up topics.

Week 2. Students mapped out a plan for their articles and visuals and began rough drafts of some articles. The research background usually provided the springboard for article ideas. We spent time in class collaborating on plans. If students had problems formulating plans, we brainstormed together on the document camera. I asked students to turn in surveys so I could conduct a few each period in order to give them the data for their visuals.

Week 3. Students shared all rough drafts with members of a group. Some students presented not only their work done to date, but also the process that had brought them there. I reminded students that cover design and the about-the-editor page were the most fun to do so, perhaps, it might be wiser to save that closer to the end. I also reminded them to finalize a Table of Contents at the end, so it would accurately reflect the pages in the magazine.

Week 4. In the remaining time I often scheduled class time in the computer lab so students who had computer issues at home or students who could not make it to the library after school could complete some work. At the same time, I collaborated with other members of the class to evaluate their progress during the final stages. Often the students who worked independently at home were excited about helping their peers at their computer stations.

Examples of Student Magazine Plans

Fashion

"Meet Stella McCartney"—fact page
"The History of Makeup"—report
"Top New Styles for Fall"—description
"Random Questions with Ralph Lauren"—interview
"The Middle School Fashion Scene"—analysis
Survey of Favorite Teen Brands Pie Chart—results

Cockroaches

"Man's Best Friend"
—persuasive essay exploding myths about cockroaches
"The Survivors"—analysis of cockroach longevity
Cockroach Poetry
"My Phobia"—true story of fear of cockoaches
"Extermination"—report on the latest in extermination
Collage of different types of cockroaches

Baseball

"Derek Jeter"—biography

"Subway Series"—Mets and Yankees comparison

"On the Bench"—analysis and description of injuries

"On Your Terms"—glossary of baseball terms

"How Much Is Enough?"—argument against players' salaries

"A Day at the Park"—narrative

Original photography of Yankee/Mets games or
survey of top ball players graph—results

Social Networking

"Facebook"—a history

"Cyberbullying"—editorial

"The Language of Texting"—a primer and how-to

"Do You Really Want to Socialize?"—pros and cons

"The Wonderful World of YouTube"—how do you define it?

"Five Platforms Teens Love"—comparison

Evolution of social networks since
the 60s in a timeline format

Tips on Writing Modes

- Continually reinforce that a magazine would be the final product, not a binder of reports.

- Bring in old magazines to show them the range of writing to include.

- Review any unfamiliar writing modes. Example
  - Fact Sheet or Did You Know—a bulleted list of facts
  - Interview—An interview would present the questions asked of an interviewee with his/her responses.
  - Q & A—To use the format to present research, the writer creates a question then synthesizes research to formulate a response.

Tips on Visuals

- If students were stuck coming up with ideas for visuals, they could create a survey about their topic, which easily translates to a chart or graph of results. For example, a fashion magazine could feature a graph showing students' favorite stores. I would do a few of the surveys at the beginning of classes as long as they were neatly typed up with places for me to record responses. This gave students lots of data.

- Students enjoyed making demo videos for projects that involved "How Tos." For example, a student creating a skateboarding magazine included a DVD demonstrating his "moves." A cheerleader showed a 5-minute video of a competition that illustrated one of the articles she had written.

Library Media Specialist's Role

From its inception, the magazine project had enthusiastic support from all of the school librarians at my school. And, the library media specialist I worked with in the latter part of my career became an integral part of the process. She presented students with sanctioned databases, was willing to get additional resources through Inter-Library Loan, and presented a workshop on MLA Format and Works Cited, and the proper use of citations.

Time to Celebrate

Sharing their projects with the class, students highlighted articles and other points of interest. Truly I have never seen students so over-the-top in terms of appreciation of a project assignment itself as well as the outstanding results of their peers. Students read these magazines for months before class began, during free periods, and later when they were on display in our library. Parents called or e-mailed to say that they had never seen such effort and motivation in their children, and they too were amazed at the phenomenal results. There is no big secret about why this happened. When students are in charge of their own learning with you as a guide and facilitator, the possibilities are endless. The diversity of topics allowed everyone to tap into a personal interest from every individual sport imaginable to sports magazines in general; fashion, modeling, hairstyles; singers, bands, and rap stars; every animal on the planet; technology tools and software; health issues, food and nutrition; teen-type magazines; television, movies, and Broadway plays; phobias, astrology, psychic phenomena...each year students would think of topics that had never been addressed before. From my vantage point, all I could do was bask in the glow of their successes.

Grading the Project

Put on GC

I gave the following rubric to the students when I assigned the project and students used it as a checklist for their ongoing work. In addition, to internalize the rubric, students practiced grading projects that my former students had left behind. ~~Because all work in the final product was in a presentation binder, I did not make corrections or "red ink" the project in any way.~~ I had students fill out large index cards with their name, magazine topic, and the three categories of the rubric. I collected all the cards by class, so when it came time to grade the project, I filled out the card with corresponding numbers to each category, then made comments and suggestions on the card.

Magazine Rubric

Appearance

4—Extremely professional in appearance; creative and appealing in design and graphics; exemplary in neatness and organization

3—Neat in appearance; appealing in design and graphics; overall well organized

2—Uneven in appearance; creative aspects appear rushed or inconsistent; lacking in organization

1—Neatness of little or no concern; no attention to creativity or design; minimal evidence of organization

Written Content

4—Uses a variety of required writing modes in articles; sophisticated vocabulary and sentence structure mechanically correct; includes all requirements of assignment

3—Uses most of the required writing modes in articles; simplistic vocabulary and sentence structure; minor distracting mechanical errors; includes all requirements of assignment

2—Overlooks use of some required writing modes in articles; obvious error in word choice, sentence structure; distracting mechanical errors affect readability; some requirements may not be addressed

1—Does not use required writing modes in articles; numerous errors in word choice and sentence structure; mechanical errors affect comprehension; many requirements are not addressed

Research/Works Cited

4—Required number of sources/correct form for Works Cited/Citations

3—Missing a source/minor inaccuracies in form

2—Not enough sources/inaccuracies in form

1—No evidence of research, no Works Cited page

Conversion of points to grades:

Total points from rubric:	Grade:
12	= 100
11	= 95
10	= 90
9	= 85
8	= 80
7	= 75
6	= 70
5	= 65
4	= 60
3	= 55

Chapter 8

"Poetry is the language in which man explores his own amazement."
—Christopher Fry

If It's Spring, It's Time for Poetry

My overriding memory of the poetry units in my own schooling is banging on the desk to pound out the "meter" of each poem as if that were the sum and substance of poetry study! Though all teachers must attend to the mechanics of poetry, there are creative ways to do so that will keep students engaged. At the middle level, a unit on poetry allows you to connect to the soul of each of your students, awakening feelings, emotions, and thus, their voices. I had great success using the following strategies.

Introduction

Use a film clip from the movie *Dead Poets' Society* in which Mr. Keating has his students rip out the introduction to their poetry text because it instructs students to treat poems antiseptically, almost mathematically, and this unorthodox instructor in a very straight-laced boarding school wants to awaken the inner poet in each of his students. He wants to tap the inner passions of these boys who are used to "by-the-book" instructors. While I am not an advocate of vandalizing texts, the message comes across loud and clear—poetry is not measured and dissected, but experienced.

Focus

While I always provided my students with the vocabulary terms of poetry because assessments demanded it and a common language facilitated our discussions, I was more focused on introducing the sheer variety of poems in hopes of countering the all too common lament of middle school students: "I hate poetry!!!" Just as there are diverse backgrounds and interests among students, there are just as many different poems that arouse their individual interests: love poems, silly poems, the questions-of-life poems, sports poems, nature poems, and so on. And by spring, I had a sense of the poems particular classes might enjoy. It also helped that we dabbled in poetry here and there along our literary way: Ponyboy Curtis and Johnny Cade discussing Robert Frost's poem "Nothing Gold Can Stay"; analyzing Edgar Allan Poe's poem "Alone" in terms of autobiographical clues; connecting "Richard Cory" to the themes of *The Outsiders*.

Demonstrate Your Interest

During our unit on poetry, I would write poems at night or during the school day—short ones, in-the-moment ones, on all different topics. I would randomly share these little ditties, and students would praise my efforts. But what I was showing them was that poems do not have to be these elaborate things that wrack the brain, but an outpouring of brain or heart activity with little restriction on form and structure.

Getting Started

Creating a Positive Impression

As soon as I would mention the word "poetry," I could be confident that the majority of my students would give it a thumbs down. I immediately knew what they didn't like about it—it was hard to figure out and even more difficult to write. Further, when I asked them what poetry is, they had a difficult time putting their thoughts into words. So I devised an exercise, in which I would have student groups synthesize their thoughts on the subject. I would give the following to each group, then record their reactions on the document camera on my template.

What Is Poetry?

Is it a jigsaw of metaphors, whispering
personifications, or similes using like or as?

Or a million plus one hyperboles?

Is it the "BOOM ! " of onomatopoeia?

Or Lego blocks of stanzas?

To the tune of Rhythm?

Meter?

Rhyme?

Perhaps,

But Poetry is

_____

_____

_____

_____

_____

_____

_____

_____

What I usually found was that students would first name the poetry techniques they had studied in their earlier grades of schooling. Once we got past that, they would begin to see beyond the techniques.

These are some of their findings:

Poetry is...

another way to communicate

what you want it to be

descriptive language

sound

concrete

free

rhyme or not

a story

emotions

feelings

fantasy

experiences

life

the soul

culture

deep

fun

a whole new world

At that point I felt we were getting somewhere! Middle school students can be victims of their own ruts—in this case that poetry was some bogeyman that haunted them. All I did was try to open their eyes a bit wider so they could explore other possibilities! Now we were on to something, and their energies were simply redirected in a more positive direction.

Word Choice/Power of Language

Use a simple word association game to show students how poets play with language, choosing words for sound, for images they suggest, for emotions they arouse. Give students a list of ten words. After the teacher says each one, students write the first thing that comes to mind: sunset, school, balloon, car, silk, clown, umbrella, red, daisy, snow. Going around the room, have students share their responses. The purpose is to have them understand the number one rule of poetry: the poet is in command, using words from his/her experience, words that capture feelings and emotion. No one can tell other students that their word associations are incorrect; the associations belong uniquely to them. And thus the lesson: poetry is freeing, not focusing on the right answer.

Vocabulary

Whenever you give students a vocabulary sheet, you run the risk of having them shut down. Explain to students that having a common vocabulary allows the class discussions to flow more smoothly, and that these terms would show up on their standardized tests! Once we looked at a few poems together and "played" with the terminology, students were engaged in identifying the various techniques, almost as though they were on a treasure hunt. I used two poems by Carl Sandburg, both simplistic, yet loaded with poetic conventions: "Fog" and "Splinter." Then I would move on to Alfred Lord Tennyson's "The Eagle"; this is a wonderful poem to analyze as a class using the common vocabulary that students were beginning to internalize. I often reinforced that by having groups of students work on poems together using their "crib sheet," and while excitement might be too strong a word, there would always be vibrant, lively discussion about a poet's use of sound and figures of speech. In addition, it takes a great deal of mindbending to identify figures of speech or recognize oxymorons or analyze appeals to the senses—this really tapped into students' critical thinking skills.

Great poems for group analysis are "Foul Shot" by Edwin A. Hoey, "The Waking" by Theodore Roethke, "Lost" by Carl Sandburg, "April" by Marcia Masters, and "The Base Stealer" by Robert Francis.

Poetry Terms

Sound Techniques

Alliteration: several words that start with the same consonant are placed close together. For example: "**P**atty **P**rice **p**icks **p**etunias and **p**ansies."

Consonance: the same consonant is repeated several times close together; unlike alliteration, the consonant may not always be at the beginning of the word, but internal or at the end. For example: "**P**i**p** **p**o**p**s **p**o**p**corn **p**atiently."

Assonance: the repetition of vowel sounds. For example: "**My eye** sp**ie**d the h**i**gh w**i**re" or "J**ea**n rec**ei**ved h**ea**ps of b**ea**ns."

Onomatopoeia: a word that sounds like what it represents.

For example: words for animal sounds, such as "**meow**" and "**oink**" are onomatopoeias, as are words like "**pop**," click, " and "**sizzle**" that sound like the noise they are naming.

Rhyme

Internal rhyme: two or more words in the same line of a poem rhyme. For example: the first line of "The Raven" by Edgar Allen Poe reads, "Once upon a midnight **dreary**, while I pondered, weak and **weary**."

End rhyme: The repetition of end sounds. For example:
> Fading light
> Dims the sight

Rhyme scheme: the pattern in which the rhyme occurs

Rhythm: the beat of a line of poetry

Figures of Speech

Metaphor: an implied comparison between two unlike things that suggests one thing is another. For example: "All the world's a stage," "Life's a short summer," "Fred is a pig at the table."

Personification: an object or animal is given human qualities. For example: Her heart cried out; the screams of trees; "Time, the subtle thief of youth."

Simile: a direct comparison between two usually unrelated things using like or as. For example: Marie eats like a bird; the ball sailed through the air like a bullet.

Hyperbole: an exaggeration for the sake of emphasis which is not to be taken literally. For example: Wild horses couldn't drag me; I could eat a cow.

Others

Imagery: descriptive language that creates pictures in the reader's mind. Certain words and comparisons are used to help the reader see, hear, feel, smell, and taste what is going on and evoke a certain mood or emotion.

Symbol: a word or image that signifies something other than what is literally represented. For example: rose= love; dove=peace.

Oxymoron: a type of paradox in which two linked words contradict each other. For example: jumbo shrimp; dress pants; pretty ugly

In this phase of poetry analysis we were not studying rhyme or alliteration or simile as isolated terms or mechanics, but as an artist's brush strokes in painting a picture. Poets rely on sound, structure, figures of speech, and imagery because their medium relies on economy of language, but at the same time, they are evoking responses from their audience.

Poet's Purpose

Students often discover for themselves that poets are highly emotional folks just like they are who have a great deal to say about life in all its aspects. Poets celebrate the wonder of nature, ask the unanswerable questions about life and death, and even teach us lessons. My students' standardized tests always included a poem, and the number one question was "What is the poet's purpose?" While some poets focus more on structure and sound techniques than they do important life lessons, I exposed my students to a variety of poems that had important themes to convey. I did this in my literature units when we explored important themes of short stories and novels, but during the poetry unit, I would share poems for thematic analysis as well.

A few favorites that would elicit lively discussion included "Birdsong" by W.S. Merwin, "Primer Lesson" and "Street Window" by Carl Sandburg, "Dust" by Sydney King Russell, and "Barter" by Sara Teasdale. And, of course, to bring us back to the fun of poetry as well as some life lessons, we would look at the collected poems of their favorite, Shel Silverstein.

At this point, I was still holding students off from writing their own poems. I created some fun exercises that elicited wonderful statements like "I love poetry" or "What cool poem do you have for us today?" I wanted to keep the momentum going and have the students exposed to all different types of poems before we settled into what I called Poetry Workshop. But I would always have students who would "jump the gun," and that became an even greater motivator than I could have imagined. If students came in with a poem or two asking me to read what they had written, with their permission, I immediately put them in the spotlight. These impromptu offerings would set the tone for another wonderful poetry class!

Poetry Fun Friday

I would choose poems that were longer and full of techniques, but most important of all, appealed to students. Using poems in a listening exercise allows students to really focus on the sounds of the poem and to hear how a poet plays with language. They can visualize the imagery and think about the poet's purpose. One of my favorites to read was "April" by Marcia Masters. It is a poem that begs to be read aloud. Masters uses many of the sound techniques and figures of speech we had studied and appeals to the senses of hearing and sight.

Another great poem for this purpose is Roald Dahl's "Little Red Riding Hood and the Wolf." Besides the aforementioned techniques, Dahl uses a bit of satire to convey his purpose which resonates with students. Other poems for this purpose are "Flight of the Roller-Coaster" by Raymond Souster, "Mushrooms" by Mary Oliver, and "Seal" by William Jay Smith.

Oxymorons

For some reason my eighth graders loved oxymorons. Perhaps, it's the contradiction in terms, which, when you think about it, is the hallmark of adolescence. From a teaching standpoint, these little nuggets are mini brain teasers that tap critical thinking. I would begin with my own list and discuss them with students, but soon thereafter, students would come barging into class with their own found lists. I would have students work in groups to analyze these lists as well as see if they could come up with their own oxymorons. I would try to get them to top my own: an almost hole-in-one (the story of my golf game).

Poetry Reading

Fortunately, I had class sets of two poetry anthologies in my classroom for this assignment. However, if I had not, I would have asked students to bring in their favorite poems to do this poetry reading. Of course, I would always prepare to have selections for those students who did not bring in a poem or have the librarian pull poetry anthologies for them to peruse. I really wanted students to find a poem that "spoke" to them. Because they were sharing these poems with the class, I wanted them to have feelings invested in the poem whatever their reasons. I would have them prepare the readings with three criteria: reading with feeling and voice, explaining what the poem meant to them, and finding some examples of the techniques from their poetry terms. I gave them a few class periods to prepare and help one another. This exercise was not so much about a grade but about the experience of owning a poem and sharing it. We could all help each other with the poetry terms and techniques. It was also a great way to expose students to a huge number and variety of poems. They loved it—no great pressure but a lot of collaboration.

Found Poetry Leads to Writing

My students loved this exercise, and it was a great lead-in to a poetry writing workshop. I would find a newspaper clipping about some bizarre incident that would capture their interest. One that comes to mind was a customer at a custard stand found the tip of a finger in his cup of custard. It turns out an employee had his finger severed at the tip, and somehow it ended up in this customer's treat. I read the article to the students, who then free wrote a poem about what they heard. The results were descriptive and comical; the students begged for more. It's not hard to find such articles these days since truth is stranger than fiction.

Poetry Workshop

I would end our poetry journey with a few days of in-class writing. At this point students were ready to take up the gambit, so to speak. Each day I would offer some topic suggestions, read some little pieces of my own, even compose some right on the spot, but students were free to explore their own inner poet. Since so much middle school writing requires that students avoid "I," I would remind them that poems were the perfect vehicle for capturing their "I point of view" about their childhoods, memories, dreams, goals, and aspirations. I was never disappointed, and even the original reluctant "poetry haters" were able to produce some wonderful pieces. Occasionally there would be a hold-out who "couldn't write poetry," so I would sit with that student and suggest some free writing about various topics. I would then take the words and give them poetic structure; together we had composed some poems! If we had time, I would take students to our computer room so they could "publish" their poems with graphics, and later, share them in the classroom on the document camera. Students were always in awe of their fellow classmates' creativity and profound insights.

The Key to Poetry Writing

I think the key to a successful poetry unit is removing obstacles and barriers to real enjoyment. Over-analysis, over-emphasis on poetic terminology, and stifling restrictions on poetry writing assignments will surely quell student voice. I never felt that I was lowering my expectations; in fact, I always exceeded them because I had liberated students from so many of their negative associations with poetry.

My final reward to my students was a huge undertaking that occupied most of my spring break, and though each year I would tell myself I would not do it again, I kept it up until retirement because I knew how much it meant to them. I would write a poem about each of my classes devoting at least four lines to each student. I would find that the more interesting "characters" of the class required many more lines, but each student was acknowledged. These were rhyming poems that captured the essence of each student, and I can still remember their surprise and appreciation that I would do this for them!

Write a poem about kids in class for fun!

respond to Ch. 10 +
create # for beginning of
year

Chapter 9

"When you come to the end of your
rope, tie a knot and hang on."
—Franklin D. Roosevelt

To the Finish Line

Poetry usually brought my classes to the last few weeks of school.
At this point, academics could become very fractured. State tests,
field trips, and school business often interrupted the flow of
classes. While middle school can be a zany place on any given day,
the weeks preceding summer vacation can be, there's no other way
to say it, "loony"! At this point some teachers were loosening up a
bit, but I kept things pretty structured mainly for my own sanity.
Spring/summer fever hits hard, especially in eighth grade, with
students worrying about "prom" dates and dresses and awaiting
the debut of the yearbook, so I would ratchet things up a bit.

I found that the little bit of extra work required was well worth the
smooth, less chaotic finale to the school year. I had many different
activities in my end-of-the-year arsenal. I chose according to the
group of students I had that year. If I felt that a particular class
needed a bit more structure, I went that way. Some classes were
able to handle working on a creative project. In my firm, "Mrs.
Scott way," I also reminded students that I was still at the helm

and responsible for their academic life until they participated in Moving Up Day.

Activities to Combat End-of-the-Year Middle School Mania

- Using a printout of all the stories and novels we had read, student groups created a five- to ten-minute review session. These could be creative such as charades or game shows or review questions or quizzes.

- Students wrote letters to the incoming eighth graders for the following school year about how to survive Mrs. Scott's English class. They could be serious or funny but they had to be informative. The winning letter would be abridged and included on my Course Outline for the following school year.

- Because all departments in my middle school were required to administer final exams, I asked students to help by creating comprehensive essay questions for possible use on the exam.

- Students reviewed their writing folders and noted growth. They wrote a self-assessment piece of their findings as well as what they discovered about themselves as writers.

- I often used my classes as "guinea pigs" to run new stories or ideas by them as well as any clips or short videos I was considering integrating into the curriculum. They loved giving thumbs up or down to different materials.

- If our computer lab was open, I had students create a mini-memory book of their years at the middle school including some or all of the following: description of a favorite teacher; telling about their most embarrassing moment; insights about what they had learned both academically and personally; most memorable field trip; a poem about the middle school experience; sharing concerns about the transition to high school. They were free to add their own topics as well. Students really enjoyed this look back and were able to take their "books" home. This was not so much about earning a grade for the project as the importance of effort and participation.

- Though students would often be tapped out when it came to writing essays and the like, they rarely tired of writing about themselves. I would have them respond to a series of prompts, then have all willing participants share: What is your most important possession? What is the best birthday present you could receive? What is the best advice you ever received? What is your favorite song? What is your worst pet peeve? What makes your friend "best"? What is something you like about yourself? Of course my students, by this time of the school year, knew they had to explain "why" for each prompt.

- Another variation on the "What" prompt is the "I Wish" prompt: I wish I could uninvent…I wish I was more like…I wish there was a law…I wish I could go…I wish everyone would learn…I wish I could transport myself to…I wish my name was…

- A wonderful gift from the outgoing students to those entering in the fall is a "book." Again like those I mentioned in previous chapters, this can be a binder of pages to which each student contributes a page. For example, I did a riff on Margaret Wise Brown's *The Important Book*, for which each student created a page about something important to them, along with descriptive details about that thing and illustrations. The same could be done for a book of literary reviews of the works we read or a book of advice on surviving the new school year. The gift givers loved the idea and those on the receiving end were already enthused the moment they walked in the door on the first day of school.

Chapter 10

"Everything is alive; everything is interconnected."
—Cicero

What About Reading and Writing Instruction?

Many middle school English Language Arts teachers are fortunate to have a block of time to teach their subject, but I had, at most, 45 minutes, five days a week. To offer a course rich in literature and full of projects that tapped students' creativity and critical thinking, I had to be imaginative about how I incorporated the all-important demanded skills of my subject area that I knew my students needed, from making inferences in reading to correcting run-on sentences in their writing.

As I said at the beginning of this book, any attempt to teach a skill in isolation rather than in context of its application is not optimal, at least in my experience. I learn most when I see relevance and interconnectedness, understand the context in which I will use the information, then apply what I have learned. For adolescents, those needs are magnified a hundredfold. Therefore, any reading strategies I offered students were given in the context of short stories and novels we were studying. Vocabulary words were examined in context rather than as isolated lists, and reading comprehension strategies were modeled and discussed as they applied to our class stories or novels. Elements of the writing process, traits of writing, and the conventions of the English language were taught in mini-lessons in tandem with actual assignments and projects. Whether I used my own writing or student writing as models, outlines and graphic organizers to illustrate process, or taught short grammar lessons based on errors, the means was always authentic rather than artificial from worksheets or packets.

Writing Instruction

Because my students started writing at the very beginning of the year, I was able to diagnose their individual problems in writing. I would use their early writing pieces to provide examples of confused word pairs, capitalization and punctuation errors, and fragments and run-ons. With student permission, I would showcase models and also examples in need of improvement. My students always felt safe because they knew we were all in this "writing thing" together. Adolescent writing is rife with redundancy, errors in subject/verb agreement, and use of informal language—I was never lacking for "real" examples in my instruction. In addition, we would work through sentence combining exercises to correct over-reliance on simple sentences, add details to statements that were too general, or search for more precise words to vary language use or practice using various transitional words. Whenever I gave an essay writing assignment, I would provide an outline or graphic organizer for the particular mode: argument, cause/effect, analysis, comparison. We would also brainstorm appropriate introductions and conclusions, the bane of many of my students. If the students were writing a creative narrative, I would teach a lesson on the use of dialogue and its proper punctuation.

In no time at all, I had many papers from which to draw wonderful examples from student work that illustrated the all-important traits of meaning, development, organization, and language use. In peer editing groups I had students use rubrics specific to writing tasks to identify strengths and weaknesses in the particular piece we were working on. Instruction about writing, therefore, was ongoing and fluid.

Refreshers

My students often needed refreshers in any or all facets of writing that I have mentioned. We all can get sloppy in our habits, and so I would repeat a mini-lesson here or there as the need would arise. I also sent the students on their way with an assignment with important reminders about what they should focus on for that particular assignment—"support with specific details," "define your voice," "watch those introductory commas."

Set Expectations

I learned early in the writing strand of my curriculum that "you get what you ask for." What you tell students beforehand about expectations, requirements, even those gentle caveats about what to avoid, reaps giant rewards when word meets paper. If you map out what you expect ahead of time, you spend much less time wagging a finger at the class about all the things "you wanted" but they did not do. Middle school students may have a sixth sense about many things, but they are not mind readers.

Reading Instruction

Reading instruction in a heterogeneously grouped ELA classroom is problematic because students are all over the map in terms of skill and comprehension. While struggling readers in my middle school received some form of remediation and my special education students were given additional support, there were still so many students who struggled with class novels for a host of reasons. Some students wanted to grab the book, read it at home, and be done. Others would beg for class time because they were slow readers, not necessarily unskilled. Others, and there are now plenty of them, do not want to read at all. Usually I gave two to three weeks for a class novel to be completed and worked on related themes and other works building up to the due date. Later on, close to mid-year, I would book talk five or six books and have students choose the one they felt appealed to them. As trust built in the classroom, students knew I would be honest with them about a recommendation since I had come to know their abilities at that point.

As mentioned in Chapter 4, the assignment I would give along with the book would always be something that fostered comprehension. The most helpful approach that I always offered as an alternative, though, was "the sticky note approach." I would give students 3 x 5 lined sticky notes, if they did not have their own. I would have them place two at the end of each chapter to record the following: characters and brief descriptions, main ideas, difficult vocabulary, mini-summaries, and questions they could not answer. Even "good" readers reported that this system was most helpful to them. I also set aside class time each day for any and all questions related to their reading as they made their way to the due date.

I would always devote the first few classes when a novel was assigned to read the first few chapters aloud. This provided a wonderful opportunity for modeling important reading strategies.

- Visualization—what were they "seeing" as we read
- Author's purpose—main ideas and identifying author's meaning
- Writer's style—how the author approaches his/her subject: literary elements, mood, word choice
- Vocabulary—using context to determine meaning
- Interpretation—making inferences; drawing conclusions
- Extending understanding—connections to personal experience, another text, or multi-media

There is no doubt in my mind that students in middle school need a block of time to explore the many strands of the English Language Arts standards. However in that I did not have that option, I tried to maximize every opportunity I had to "build in" reading, writing, and critical thinking instruction. I am also happy to say that more and more schools are having ELA teachers work with content area teachers to foster more reading and writing in their subject areas as well as offer professional development in the areas of reading and writing in the content area. Teachers, in general, are now focusing on student work and offering writing strategies to students specific to their own subject areas. There is great dialogue going on about the kinds of reading that students are exposed to in their other coursework. The added bonus is that students are getting healthy doses of non-fiction works in those subjects freeing up the English Language Arts teacher to hold on to the literature that truly does awaken the middle school voice!

Some Final Thoughts…

"It is the supreme art of the teacher to awaken joy in creative expression and knowledge."
—Albert Einstein

Recently I spoke to education candidates at a local college about my book *Secrets from the Middle: Making Who You Are Work for You* and about highly effective teaching in general. I told these students that so many of us lose our teaching "souls" because we are mired in increased pressures, expectations, mandates, and new initiatives. Because old habits die hard in this retired English teacher, I had a prop along with me to make a point. I took out an artichoke to demonstrate the many layers of teacher responsibility today that must be peeled away to reveal the tender heart. However, highly effective teachers never lose sight of the heart of what they do, day in and day out. Those of us fortunate to teach English Language Arts do not have to dig too deeply to find interesting, engaging, relevant materials that provide opportunities for student interaction and elicit enthusiastic responses from not only their minds but also their tender hearts!

As I said to my audience, I learned early on that the only person I could control in the education community was ME—not my students, not their parents, not administrators. How I led in the classroom was with passion and love, how I chose materials was with passion and love, and clearly that was reciprocated by my students. If the offerings you bring to the table bring you joy, your students will follow suit.

My last bit of advice for the soon-to-be teachers in my audience was to make sure they celebrate those joys more: true joy is in students' successes whether they be critical insights, amazing writing, beyond-expectations projects, or the sounds of collaboration and excitement. It is so easy to go down the negative path of stresses and pressures that all teachers experience today; thus, it has never been more important to CELEBRATE!

CPSIA information can be obtained
at www.ICGtesting.com
Printed in the USA
FFOW03n1413121116
29220FF